BOLLYWOOD

BOLLYWOOD

SOCIOLOGY GOES TO THE MOVIES

RAJINDER KUMAR DUDRAH

SAGE PUBLICATIONS
NEW DELHI • THOUSAND OAKS • LONDON

Copyright © Rajinder Kumar Dudrah, 2006

First published in 2006 by

Sage Publications India Pvt Ltd
B-42, Panchsheel Enclave
New Delhi 110 017
www.indiasage.com

Sage Publications Inc
2455 Teller Road
Thousand Oaks
California 91320

Sage Publications Ltd
1 Oliver's Yard
55 City Road
London EC1Y 1SP

Published by Tejeshwar Singh for Sage Publications India Pvt Ltd, typeset in 10.5/12.6 Souvenir LT BT at InoSoft Systems, Noida, and printed at Chaman Enterprises, New Delhi.

Library of Congress Cataloging-in-Publication Data

Dudrah, Rajinder Kumar.
Bollywood: sociology goes to the movies/Rajinder Kumar Dudrah.
    p. cm.
    Includes bibliographical references and index.
  1. Motion pictures—India—Social aspects. 2. Motion picture industry—India—Bombay. I. Title.

PN1993.5.I8D83   302.23'430954—dc22   2006   2005037855

ISBN: 0-7619-3460-X (Hb)   81-7829-610-1 (India-Hb)
        0-7619-3461-8 (Pb)   81-7829-611-X (India-Pb)

Sage Production Team: Sunaina Dalaya, Rajib Chatterjee and Santosh Rawat

FOR MY MUM AND DAD
AND
SURINDER, BALVINDER, MEENA AND PINKY,
FOR ALWAYS BEING THERE.

CONTENTS

LIST OF ILLUSTRATIONS

ACKNOWLEDGEMENTS

I am grateful to the Arts and Humanities Research Council (AHRC) for funding the research for this book with travel money and with a grant from the Research Leave Scheme. I am also grateful to the School of Arts, Histories and Cultures at the University of Manchester for additional travel funds and for allowing me to take a sabbatical.

I, along with my co-researcher and colleague Dr Amit Rai of Florida State University, USA, thank the British Academy for the grant from their Joint International Activities Research Scheme to help us carry out our research work for Chapter 4 in New York City, USA.

I also take this opportunity to thank Amit for allowing me to draw on a version of our joint research and writing for Chapter 4 (which will appear in a revised form in the journal *New Cinemas*, 3 [2], 2005). Thank you for being a good co-researcher and generator of intellectual dialogue. I have enjoyed our conversations about thinking through Bollywood cinema as an assemblage.

The staff at the following libraries have been most helpful: the British Film Institute's Library, London, and also at the Lenagan Library at the University of Manchester. Special thanks to Kirsty Deloose and to Gary Penrice at the Lenagan Library.

Colleagues, staff and students in the School of Arts, Histories and Cultures at the University of Manchester—thanks for listening, critiquing and contributing and for being supportive of my teaching and research.

I also wish to acknowledge here, Heather Tyrrell, for allowing me to draw on our joint work. A version of Chapter 2 was originally co-written by us and is to appear in E. Tincknell and I. Conrich (eds), *Film's Moments of Musical Performance* (Forthcoming, Edinburgh University Press). The latest chapter here, is a revised and an extended and developed argument and has been written by myself. Thanks to Dr Sangita Gopal and to Dr Sujata Moorti for their feedback on Chapter 5.

I thank the staff at Sage Publications for their helpful editorial advice and inputs. Thanks to Chris Rojek, Mila Steele and to Sandra Tharumalingam, Tejeshwar Singh, Ritu Vajpeyi-Mohan, Sunanda Ghosh, and to Sunaina Dalaya. Thank you also to the two anonymous Sage readers from India and the UK for their insightful comments on a draft of the manuscript.

My undergraduate and postgraduate tutors have been exemplary scholars in cultural and social research and I am grateful for their inspiration and for reading various drafts of this work, whether at the proposal stage or in terms of actual chapters. In this respect I extend my gratitude to Professors Sue Harper, Keith Tester, John Gabriel, and to Dr Gargi Bhattacharyya. I am also grateful to the following people—good friends, providers of information, pillars of support and senders of good wishes— for supporting me during isolated periods of writing: Lloyd Williams, Tarlowchan and Sangita Dubb, Dr Malika Mehdid, Kelly Rheam (Princess of Fire), Dr Malcolm Dick, Andrew Craydon, Sunny Lochab (for funky dance floor moves and for additional flexible data storage ideas), Sanjeev Chauhan (for help with preparing image stills), Moti Gokulsing, Dr Jigna Desai (for advice on the preparation of stills) and Dr Gita Rajan.

I am indebted to my Gurus—Sant Niranjan Dass ji, Sant Ramanand ji, and Sant Surinder Dass ji—who reside in Dera Sant Sarwan Dass, Ballan, Punjab, India, and who have been extremely kind with their guidance and blessings: *Naam teri ki jot lagaye.* My parents, older brother (Raj Mulk), and sisters have been anchors of support and have given me much needed love throughout my work. They have also provided me with many opportunities to discuss at length the ideas put forward in this book. A special thank you to my 'li'l bro' Manoj Dudrah for being grown-up when I am not, and for being my most intelligent critic. My acknowledgements would not be complete without mentioning my nieces and nephews who have all contributed (directly and indirectly) to this work with their indiosyncracies, warm hugs, and by being excellent purveyors of Bollywood knowledge: Raveeta, Lukvinder, Saveeta, Inderjeet, Meenakshi, Kaveeta, Sukhvinder, Govinder, Sunil, Simerjeet, Aajay, Aaron, Rahul, Baldev and Sonia. Here's to all your diasporic adventures yet to come.

INTRODUCTION

This book intends to take the subject of sociology to the movies. More specifically, it is an attempt at rejuvenating a dormant dialogue within sociology about grasping the possible relationships between cinema, culture and society through an interdisciplinary conversation with studies of the cinema from film and media, and cultural studies. An ambitious cross-disciplinary undertaking no less, but nothing ventured nothing gained. The case study for elaboration and analysis is Bollywood—the popular Hindi cinema from Mumbai (formerly Bombay), India.

From the outset I want to be clear, I am less interested in offering a systematic and exhaustive interpretation of Bollywood cinema through the canon of founding figures of the discipline and their classical sociological theories and methods alone. This would only lead to a reductive registering of the cinema through a list of 'he said, he said' (the founding figures of sociology are often referred to as the founding fathers), which might usefully prove or disprove further, certain aspects of traditional sociology as it is put to use in the analysis of a popular cinema such as Bollywood. Rather, I am more concerned with resurrecting and extending an exciting aspect of sociological analysis and discussion that has been largely left undeveloped, that of the study of cinema and its possible relationships in culture and society. In order to reignite that debate I choose to leave aside the founding figures as tenets of the discipline, i.e., to be followed strictly, and turn instead to the creative possibility within sociology that fosters a desire to grasp with the modern social world through the application of its imagination; specifically, a sociological imagination applied to Bollywood cinema.

In the pages that follow that sociological imagination is indebted to C. Wright Mills, and is elaborated on further through a dialogue between Norman Denzin's sociology of cinema (who engages with Mill's sociological imagination), and the work of Indian and other scholars of popular Hindi cinema. The sociological imagination that is taken up and developed in this book is one that is concerned with the private and public issues of the day, writ large through the silver screen and popular cultures of Bollywood cinema. The sociological imagination as it is put to use here also engages with cinema and its related popular cultures qualitatively in order to decipher aspects of culture and social change in and around Bollywood cinema in the contemporary moment. *Sociology Goes to the Movies*, then, is an exploration of some of the dynamics, possibilities and tensions inherent in the workings of cinema as a global industry, films as popular cultural texts, and the relationships that are possible between cinema and its audiences. It is argued that this is a possible and necessary undertaking for sociology in conjunction and in dialogue with theoretical and analytical frameworks from film, media and cultural studies. What emerges then is a dialogic engagement with different yet related spheres of intellectual modes of enquiry that do not pretend to create a single, linear or uniform sociological understanding of cinema and instead work by illustrating the intersections where sociology, film, media and cultural studies can be usefully put to work together.

As a starting point, in researching and writing about Bollywood cinema in 2005 I am pleased that it appears to have arrived on the international stage, that it is almost recognised as a prolific and important world cinema. At the beginning of the new millennium Bollywood cinema's exposure became noticeably international. For example, the annual International Indian Film

Awards (IIFA) were held in London at the Millennium Dome in 2000. The international press coverage and film industry media were discussing Bollywood cinema's potential as a viable alternative to Hollywood. Building on this momentum the Bollywood film *Lagaan* (dir. Ashutosh Gowariker, 2001) was entered in the Best Foreign Film category at the Oscars, the film *Devdas* (dir. Sanjay Leela Bhansali, 2002) was featured at the Cannes Film Festival, and Bollywood films began to regularly appear in the UK Top 10 and in the US Top 20 box-office listings ahead of many big budget Hollywood blockbusters. In 2002 the British Film Institute (BFI), London, launched its Imagine Asia series with films from the South Asian subcontinent in which the screening of its Bollywood films proved very popular. From the US and Canada respectively, Mira Nair's *Monsoon Wedding* (2002) and Deepa Mehta's *Bollywood/Hollywood* (2002) brought together the aesthetics of Bollywood and Hollywood cinema together for crossover audiences. Bollywood references were also prevalent in mainstream Hollywood films such as *Moulin Rouge* (dir. Baz Luhrman, 2001). The fascination for all things Bollywood seeped into mainstream Western music, theatre, fashion, television and the high street department stores of the West (see Chapter 5). Channel 4 in Britain aired the programme *Bollywood Star* during the summer months of 2004, shortlisting six British Asian finalists from the hundreds who had entered and auditioned. The competition allowed the winner a role in one of Bollywood veteran Mahesh Bhatt's forthcoming films. Much to the surprise of the programme's audiences the winner was not a stereotypically slim or pretty girl or a handsome boy, but a large woman from Birmingham, England—Rupak Mann.[1] Towards the close of 2004 Gurinder Chadha remade Jane Austen's novel *Pride and Prejudice* for the screen as *Bride and Prejudice* in explicit Bollywood terms (see Chapter 6). And, on 26 March 2005, the non-terrestrial Zee TV channel aimed at global South Asian audiences held its Zee Cinema Awards at the Excel Arena in London's Docklands and broadcast this award ceremony throughout its television network.[2] Perhaps this list of Bollywood cinema's arrival is fast growing.

However, the sociological imagination whilst taking note of recent developments on the cultural and social landscape also alerts us to probe further and inspect closer at what appears to be going on. We need to exercise a little caution, as all is not what it seems in the celebration of Bollywood cinema in recent times. Prior to the jubilations of Bollywood's arrival in the international media this was a cinema often ridiculed and marginalised by the Western media and elitist academics for being mass escapist entertainment and trivial. Not that these uninformed populist criticisms have gone away but that their focus has shifted as Bollywood has 'arrived' on the international media stage. The question is: how and why?

Furthermore, Bollywood's recent incarnation as global popular culture has been discussed by some as part of a cosmopolitan-celebration attitude, particularly in Britain and in the US, that gives increased visibility to Bollywood cinema and diasporic South Asians as chic and 'in' (e.g., Desai 2004: 40–69). Yet, this visibility is occurring simultaneously with the heightened processes following the globalisation of the events of 9/11 in New York and 7 July in London where people with brown skin, and Muslims in particular, are increasingly under surveillance and are being racialised. Hence, this visibility is accompanied by a bifurcation in which 'South Asianness' is hip, cool and British, and South Asians themselves are dangerous and foreign (ibid.: 68). We therefore need to be careful about simply going along with multicultural celebrations of Bollywood cinema in which it is commodified for safe consumption and in which the possible cultural politics of its films are often ignored. We need to further ask and examine what these politics might be and where they lead to in cultural and social terms through the films, their related popular cultures, and their audiences. In the dialogue that is put forward across the disciplines of sociology, film, media, and cultural studies, *Sociology Goes to the Movies* intends to illustrate and elaborate on such moments.

In terms of the limitations of the scope of this book, it primarily focuses on the urban Indian and diasporic South Asian audience experiences of Bollywood cinema. Nonetheless, this should not preclude others to examine the multiple dimensions of popular Hindi cinema audiences, not least rural audiences, or non-Indian or non-South Asian audiences in different parts of the world for example. Where possible I have made reference to these different constituencies of the Bollywood cinematic experience. Overall, however, I have attempted to write from a vantage point, being located as an avid third-generation British South Asian consumer of Hindi films as one aspect of my cultural identity, and leave it to the readers of this work to take issue with the insights, cultural criticisms and analyses offered as whether appropriate or not.

In Chapter 1, then, let us begin by initiating the dialogue between sociology and other studies of the cinema, and make clearer the aims and layout of this book as sociology goes to the movies.

TOWARDS A SOCIOLOGY OF CINEMA

SOCIOLOGY OF CINEMA: AN OVERVIEW

Perhaps of all the areas of culture and society explored within the discipline of sociology, the topic of cinema has been less comprehensively served. Whilst there has been an ongoing exploration of the sociology of the mass media, more generally the study of cinema has been accorded sporadic attention.

Andrew Tudor (1998) offers a useful account of the sociology of cinema in the United States (US) and in Western Europe and it is worth summarising that history here. Early sociological studies of the cinema can be traced back to the twenties and thirties in the US. Fuelled by public concern in the US at the end of the twenties, the Payne Fund financed a series of research projects that brought together sociologists and social psychologists to explore the impact of motion pictures upon youth (for example, Bulmer 1933; Peterson and Thurstone 1936). The Payne Fund Studies set the tone for interwar and post-war sociological approaches to film. They were primarily concerned with the measurable effects of film on particular social categories of audience, with particular focus being made on the perceived negative effects of film in changing behaviour amongst young people.

By the forties and fifties, and across both sides of the Atlantic, mass communications research became the dominant paradigm under which popular culture came to be studied and the early sociological approaches to cinema also took shelter under this umbrella of work. Mass communications research was increasingly concerned to measure the effects of the media as symptoms of modern society as a 'mass society' (Brooker and Jermyn 2002; Swingewood 1977). Common assumptions put forward by mass society theorists, and taken up by its researchers, included notions that mass culture was crude and that its consumers were little more than undiscriminating dupes who were being injected with, and taking on board, media messages wholesale. The mass society thesis set up a framework for sociological analysis that failed to examine both the variations within the audience and the polysemy of many popular cultural texts, thereby neglecting the complexity of the cinematic apparatus.

By the sixties the mass culture and society thesis came under sustained attack with the onset of structuralism and semiology that sought to re-evaluate Hollywood films by film critics, first in France and then in Britain. For a short while there was a genuine possibility for film studies and sociology to begin to share its analyses of cinema across aesthetic, theoretical and methodological lines (cf. Wollen 1969). This alliance, however, was not taken up seriously as sociology and film studies began to diverge by the late sixties due to intellectual differences around the perceived lack of a reflective empiricism in sociology by film theorists (Tudor 1998: 192).

The seventies witnessed the mushrooming of screen theory in a direction that gave more credence to close text-based analyses of film. This kind of work was particularly prolific in the journal *Screen* of the period (see, for example, the selected chapters in Kuhn and Stacey 1999 on this history). Here, analysis tended to focus on the language of film and less attention was paid towards developing an understanding of the context in which film texts were made and comprehended. Thus, less scope was made available to adequately think about individual spectators or social structures in early semiotic accounts of cinema. When the social dimension was brought into theoretical analyses of film it was made not through the application of sociological theories or methods but instead through the concept of ideology, borrowing most notably from Lacanian-derived Althusserian approaches where the subject of cinema is considered as constituted by and through the film text (i.e., film as an example of a system of discourse) and is thereby caught within ideology. By focusing on the textual constitution of subjects, seventies film theory encouraged a method based in structural psychoanalysis rather than allowing emphasis to be placed on social contextual issues which would have enabled a more sociological approach. Thus, the terms of film theoretical discourse that became commonplace during the seventies and eighties relegated sociological considerations to the periphery.

Over the past 30 years and more there have been sporadic attempts to consider film through sociological examination, but these have been far and few between. The academic studies of Jarvie (1970) and Tudor (1974) were social accounts of Hollywood and European cinemas in terms of key films and as attempts at understanding the social role and function of cinema and its film-makers. Both were more interested in the social contextual concerns of cinematic exploration and accorded less attention to questions of aesthetics or textual analysis. The sociology of film offered neither by Jarvis nor Tudor has not been followed by others. However, repeated calls for a return to, and renewal of, the sociology of film have been made in disparate journal articles (for example, Alfonsi 1999; Dowd 1999; Pendergast 1986).

Since the eighties and nineties the rise of media and cultural studies as academic disciplines in their own right have provided an intellectual space for more complex and sophisticated accounts of texts, audiences, and their social context and relations to be articulated more fully, wherein sociologically informed researchers have been able to contribute further to understandings of film.[1]

Norman Denzin's Sociology of Cinema

In this vein, one academic who has perhaps almost exclusively been putting forward a sociology of cinema is Norman Denzin, Professor of Sociology and Communications, in *Images of Postmodern Society* (1991) and *The Cinematic Society* (1995). In the former, Denzin studies the postmodern self and its representations in two sites: in postmodern social theory, and in a select number of contemporary mainstream Hollywood movies (Denzin 1991). Here, Denzin concerns himself with examining how contemporary US and other

Western societies come to view themselves through the signs and images available to them through cinema, which itself is a refraction and an emblem of wider culture and society across race, gender and sexual lines. In particular, Denzin draws on the sociological imagination of C. Wright Mills (1959) and puts it to use in his analysis of Hollywood cinema (Denzin 1991: Chapter 4). Simply put, the sociological imagination is one that intervenes in the modern cultural and social spheres of life by questioning the common sense assumptions about these areas of activity and probing them further. Mills' sociological imagination was originally concerned with the distinction between the personal troubles that occur in the immediate worlds of experience of interacting individuals and the public issues of social structure. Mills theorised that personal troubles are often to do with the self, its emotionality, its life-projects, and its relations with others; troubles are personal matters which spill over into families and groups and they occur in the immediate social context of the person. Public issues, on the other hand, transcend personal troubles. They have to do 'with the organization of many such milieux into the institutions of an historical society' (Mills 1959: 8). They involve the social, economic, moral and cultural fabrics of a society and the ways in which these fabrics 'overlap and interpenetrate to form the larger structure of social and historical life' (ibid.). Public issues, then, are matters that often involve a perceived crisis in current institutional arrangements that threaten cherished values. Denzin considers the personal and collective social struggles organised around the personal experiences and social structures of race, gender and sexuality as brought to life in Hollywood cinema.

Developing these concerns through to *The Cinematic Society*, Denzin (1995) argues how the US has become a cinematic culture and society. Taking as his starting point Thomas Edison's invention of the kinetograph through to the start of mass cinema going in the nineteen hundreds, to the advent of sound in the twenties, to the setting up of the Hollywood studio system by the thirties, Denzin is concerned with how, over three decades, American society became a cinematic culture—a culture which came to know itself, collectively and individually, through the images and stories that Hollywood produced. Denzin alerts us to the type of viewer that has been constructed in a cinematic society, a kind of social voyeur who is often privileged across race, gender and sexual lines. At the heart of Denzin's argument, then, in *The Cinematic Society* is a concern to consider who is looking at whom, and why. And, how and why is it through cinema that particular kinds of representations about gender, race and sexuality continue to hold sway. Together, Denzin's two publications can be considered as explicit attempts at taking up an alliance and fostering a cross-disciplinary dialogue between sociological studies of cinema (i.e., why the study of cinema matters in a society), film studies (where close attention is paid to the analysis of film texts) and cultural studies (where questions of representation and power are elaborated by way of reference to ethnographic observations of the cultural and social dimensions of cinema).

Before moving on to consider the merits of Denzin's sociology of film as in conversation with existing studies of Bollywood cinema let us consider the development of the study of Indian cinema from scholars writing within and outside India, as this rich body of work has also drawn on developments in Western cultural and social theory to illuminate the mosaic that is popular Hindi cinema.

Indian Scholars and Popular Hindi Cinema

Early scholarly studies in India, whilst offering an overview of the history and development of its popular Hindi cinema, considered it to be an escapist fantasy for a mass audience. They further followed theoretical models broadly based around the Frankfurt school view of mass culture and society as standardised and ideologically deceptive (for example, Das Gupta 1981, 1991; Rangoonwalla 1975; Valicha 1988). Western film criticism also paid scant scholarly attention to Indian cinema and, when it did, it was accorded a marginal and patronising status along the aforementioned lines (for example, Cook 1996: 861). By the mid-nineties a number of studies began to emerge, both in and beyond India, that began to offer more complex accounts of the relationship of the cinema, filmic texts and its audiences; partly informed by the development of film, media and cultural studies as fields of academic study, and partly as a rebuff to simple analyses of popular Indian cinema (for example, Chakravarty 1996; Dissanayake 1994; Dissanayake and Sahai 1992; Dwyer 2000; Ganti 2004; Gopalan 2002; Kaur and Sinha 2005; Kazmi 1999; Mishra 2002; Nandy 1998; Prasad 1998; Rajadhyaksha 1998; Thomas 1985; Vasudevan 2000; Virdi 2003).[2]

In contradistinction to the development of Western film theory, Indian film theory followed lines of flight that were more readily inclusive of the social and political dimensions of cinema within India.[3]

Ashish Rajadhyaksha (1998) highlights three phases in the development of popular Indian film theory. The first phase is concerned with the films of the seventies, commonly regarded as a well-researched socio-political area, wherein India as a nation state underwent a series of domestic and international crises culminating in the declaration of national emergency by the then Prime Minister, Indira Gandhi, in 1975. The second phase is accredited to the formal entry of post-colonial theory in the mid to late eighties and the reinvestigation of the history of Indian nationalism that was opened up via a biography of the nation state. Scholars and historians conducting work that came to be known as subaltern studies (for example, Chaterjee 1986), and also the interdisciplinary arts- and humanities-based work submitted to the *Journal of Arts and Ideas* in India, are two examples of this phase. The third phase is the opening up and introduction of film studies in India through various postgraduate departments that led to the growing acceptance of film studies in previously orthodox literature, history and social science departments.

Consequently, existing scholarship on popular Indian cinema has proceeded along the following axes: audience identificatory processes (for example, Dwyer 2000; Mishra 2002; Nandy 1998; Vasudevan 2000); cinema as an ideological apparatus (Kazmi 1999; Prasad 1998); and, film as a national archive (Chakravarty 1996; Virdi 2003). Furthermore, and in ways that are not too dissimilar from Denzin's sociologically imaginative engagement with mainstream US cinema and society, the critical work of recent scholars of Bollywood cinema have also interpreted its role in the formation of a national consciousness that sets into play dominant and subordinate Indian and South Asian subcontinental identities in an uneasy and complex relationship that begs further questioning and analysis. Such identities include, for example, the representations of religion, caste and gender; the Muslim minority in India; India's relationship with its political neighbours; corruption in public life and so forth. Of note here too, is that as in the development of film studies in the West, the history of contemporary Hindi film theory also lacks an explicit engagement with issues of sociological method. But why should this matter?

TOWARDS A SOCIOLOGY OF BOLLYWOOD CINEMA

Perhaps this would be an appropriate moment to pause and make clear the hitherto implicit question that has been running throughout the previous pages—why is a sociology of cinema being advocated? Moreover, why is a sociology of Bollywood cinema being considered and what might it entail? In response to these two questions, I would like to introduce summaries of two conversations that I had in the summer of 2004: one with a radio programme producer working for a national media broadcaster, and another with a university sociology lecturer, both in the city of Manchester, UK.

In the first exchange the producer had got in touch with me as he was in the process of getting ready to go to Mumbai, India, to record a programme in which he wanted to explore Hindu nationalism and its reception amongst audiences in Bollywood movies. In our initial conversation we chatted at length over the phone, for about some 20 minutes, in which duration we discussed topics ranging from the historical emergence of popular Hindi cinema to its global outreach in the present day. The producer seemed quite keen to put forward the argument that Hindi cinema was escapism for the masses and had troubling levels of right wing and conservative politics enshrined in its movies. During the phone conversation I suggested that he might offer a more complex argument than this, as should he persist in his line of reasoning he would be producing a programme that was outdated in its thinking and simplistic in its analysis. I suggested that in addition to these aspects of Bollywood films there was a need to think through what we might mean by cinema as escapism, and whether or not the conservative politics of the films were being taken on board wholesale by Indian audiences. I invited him to a seminar at the University of Manchester in which my colleague and co-researcher, Dr Amit Rai of Florida State University, and I were giving a work in progress paper on the findings of our Bollywood cinema going research in New York City (see Chapter 4). The seminar was scheduled a few days before the producer was to make his trip to India. He and I felt that perhaps his attending the seminar might be useful for us both as a dialogue around thinking about Bollywood cinema and its audience in more complex ways. The radio producer attended and listened to our talk. During the question and answer session his familiar agenda appeared again, and he went as far as to say that we were according too much importance to the popular Hindi cinema of India as, for him, it amounted to no more than 'fluffy masala' and 'dreamlike' and 'escapist' movies.

In the conversation with the sociology lecturer during an informal drinks gathering one summer evening, my research interests into the cultural and social importance of popular film, particularly Bollywood, were being seriously challenged. He considered them to be secondary to 'proper' and 'serious' sociological research. For him, sociological research was quantitatively defined—'How many people go to the cinema everyday in India? How can you determine that cinema impacts on everyday Indians?' He even suggested that my interest in Bollywood was fine for now as long as I remembered to move on to do 'serious' social research that engaged with actual subjects and community-based organising and social movements.

The summaries of both these conversations reveal instances of the longstanding populist criticisms often directed at popular cinema and Bollywood films in particular. They also suggest a kind of unease with the emerging study of Bollywood cinema that is attempting to set about new directions in film criticism and social and cultural analysis that do away with exactly these kinds of uninformed allegations. The comments made by the radio producer illustrate a viewpoint, long held within Western and conservative interpretations about Bollywood cinema and its audiences, as patronising and unable to develop a serious engagement with the popular Hindi cinematic form. The producer appeared to have a pre-existing agenda about Bollywood cinema that he wanted to prove, rather than set out on a programme of exploration and discovery. The fact that I was suggesting another viewpoint as a different possibility to think about Bollywood cinema unsettled him and hence his retort of 'fluffy masala' movies. Interestingly, during my exchange with the producer he admitted that he hadn't seen very many Bollywood films at all.

The comments made by my colleague in sociology however perhaps surprised me more, not least because of his limiting version of what constituted cultural and social research, but more so because of his lack of a sociological imagination to consider more widely the topics of socio-cultural research. For him, a focus on social move-ments and actual social subjects are the fabric of 'good' and 'serious' sociology. Yet, funnily enough, he is unable to think about Bollywood cinema along such lines. In a response to these two conversations, themselves illustrations of ongoing and over-stressed alleged criticisms of popular Hindi cinema, I wish to highlight in this book the need to counter and move way from such commentaries and, perhaps more importantly, to situate the study of cinema, and in this case Bollywood cinema, in relation to cultural and sociological inquiry that demonstrates explicitly the role and nature of the cinematic form as part and parcel of cultural and social processes and elaborated on, although not exclusively, through an engagement with actual social subjects too.

What this book aims to do, then, is to reinvigorate and continue the dialogue that was initiated about 30 years ago and taken up sporadically across the disciplines of sociology, film and media studies, and cultural studies. Which brings us back to consider how the sociological imagination applied to cinema by Denzin (1991, 1995) can be usefully considered alongside and brought into dialogue with contemporary cultural and social studies of popular Hindi cinema. Using the example of Bollywood cinema as a social, cultural and media phenomenon, *Sociology Goes to the Movies* intends to offer aesthetic, cultural and social analyses of the cinematic form through the interdisciplinary subject enquiries of related fields in the arts, humanities and social sciences; namely across the aforementioned academic subject areas. The use of interdisciplinary and critical theoretical and methodological frameworks—germane to the subjects of sociology, film and media studies, and cultural studies— are selectively used in an attempt to establish and elaborate on some of the relationships between cinema and culture and society through the case study of Bollywood. Thus, a contemporary sociology of cinema that is put forward in this study is one that draws on interdisciplinary schools of thought and that addresses cinema in terms of its workings as a global industry, films as popular cultural texts, and the relationships that film fosters with its audiences. In essence, this book aims to view Bollywood cinema through an interdisciplinary sociological and cultural lens that argues for and suggests the need to think sociologically about cinema. Put another way, it advocates the need to think imaginatively about cinema as a global industry, films as popular cultural texts, and the relationships that are possible between cinema and its audiences. By taking sociology to the cinema, and vice versa, it is argued that we need to look at the range of intellectual and interdisciplinary possibilities that are available to us in order to renew a dialogue between sociology and studies of the cinema, thereby reviving the possibilities of how we might be able to think imaginatively about sociology and cinema. In other words, how might we be able to think about what happens to the analysis of Bollywood cinema through sociological enquiry? And, what happens to sociology when it considers a complex social, cultural and media phenomenon such as Bollywood cinema? These are two questions that we will need to revisit in the concluding chapter.

Let us now consider the remit of this book by outlining the aspects of Bollywood cinema that are taken up for comment and analysis through cultural and sociological enquiry in the pages that follow. First, what exactly might we mean when using the term 'Bollywood'?

WHAT IS 'BOLLYWOOD'?

Bollywood, the moniker for popular Hindi cinema from Mumbai, India, has become an important catchword in the vocabulary of global South Asian popular culture. Bollywood not only signifies the large number of films made and viewed in the city of Mumbai (estimated at around 200 films annually), but also the distribution, subtitling, dubbing and watching of these motion pictures worldwide. Bollywood films are viewed in all of South Asia, Africa (including the Maghreb countries of North Africa), South America, Eastern Europe and Russia (Kasbekar 1996: 366). These films are also imported to all the major metropolitan cities with sizable diasporic South Asian populations through cinema halls, and into homes via non-terrestrial cable and satellite channels. Bollywood is only one of several regional film centres within Indian cinema. Nonetheless, given its broad-based language appeal—i.e., Hindi—and the fact that it has been subtitled and dubbed into several Asiatic and European languages (more than any of India's other cinemas) makes it by far the most popular.

Outside South Asia and its diasporas, the popularity of Bollywood films in developing countries such as Nigeria, Egypt and Zanzibar has been attributed to the ways in which some of its themes and representations of Indian rural traditions and urban modernity, as coming to terms with one another, are seen as culturally familiar (Larkin 1997; Power and Mazumdar 2000). Furthermore, popular Indian cinema's characteristics of melodramatic oral performance (for example, the Hindu mythologicals and religious tales of the

Mahabharata as recounted in the genre of post-1947 independent Bollywood social dramas) have been offered as an explanation of why Hindi films would engage global audiences of similar orally-transmitted narratives (Nayar 2004).[4] In this way, Bollywood is more than just popular Hindi cinema for Indians alone. Millions of people, besides Indians and other South Asians, partake in, derive pleasure and construct social meanings from this cinema. Throughout this book, then, whilst it is acknowledged that India is the primary intended audience for Bollywood films, we need to take into further account how Bollywood cinema equally and simultaneously appeals to wider audience constituencies, not least the audiences in South Asia and its diasporas. *Sociology Goes to the Movies* specifically addresses Bollywood's popularity not only in India but also across its imagined South Asian diasporic audiences.

The viewing of Bollywood films also entails the consumption of other related cultural products that are mass produced in demand to the popularity of the Bollywood media phenomenon. These include the ensuing film music albums sold in hundreds of thousands across the world; readership of several international film magazines such as *Cineblitz*, *Movie* and *Stardust* with film reviews, gossip and star profiles; film posters and postcards; and, the countless number of electronic pages on the worldwide web with Bollywood pictures and texts which incorporate fanzines for the adoration of favourite films, actors and actresses. Bollywood film stars, singers and musicians appear together each year in entertainment shows in the metropolitan cities of the South Asian diaspora such as at the NEC Arena in Birmingham, UK. These shows comprise actors singing, dancing and re-enacting favourite film scenes and dialogues to packed and excited audiences. During 28–29 August 2004, for example, a few of the current favourite Bollywood stars Shahrukh Khan, Preity Zinta, Rani Mukherjee, Saif Ali Khan, Arjun Rampal, and Priyanka Chopra appeared in Birmingham and at the Wembley Arena in London for a weekend of shows, entitled Temptation 2004.[5] Ticket prices ranged from £15 to £55, and with the V.I.P tickets (including an after show meet with the stars) costing much more. Such shows have elaborately followed in the footsteps of earlier Bollywood stars who visited England for the first Indian Film Festival in 1957. The 'legends' of fifties Bollywood—Guru Dutt, Mehboob Khan, Nargis, Nutan, Shammi Kapoor, Waheeda Rehman and others—all came, arousing excitement that was akin to going to see The Beatles or Elvis in concert (Bhuchar 1996: 90).

Bollywood film songs are also an important part of the scheduling of South Asian radio broadcasting played daily and for several hours on radio stations throughout the diaspora. Bollywood video outlets, popularly known as 'Asian video shops', are abundant. In Britain alone, in the late nineties, it was estimated that there were over 4,000 video outlets catering to the regular demand for Bollywood films (Network East 1997). Furthermore, Bollywood movie houses like the Piccadilly Cinema on Stratford Road in Birmingham (UK) run by local South Asian entrepreneurs have mushroomed since the mid nineties regularly featuring the latest releases on the big screen. The mainstream cinema chains of Odeon, UCI and Virgin in the UK also show Bollywood films, thereby cashing in on the popularity of the movies. For example, the CineWorld multi-screen complex, Wolverhampton (UK), has been daily showing one of the latest Bollywood movies since 1995. However, the history of Bollywood film viewing in Britain dates as far back as 1926, when King George V and Queen Mary held a command performance of *Prem Sanyas* (Light of Asia) at Windsor Castle. This film was made in 1925 and co-directed by the Indo-German team of Himansu Rai and Franz Osten (Bhuchar 1996: 89).

Despite their popularity, Bollywood films are also a source of derision for some South Asians and non-South Asians alike. Common labels hurled at Bollywood films include 'unrealistic, emotional and over the top', and, 'formulaic entertainment for the masses'. Bollywood movies are often constructed as an amorphous mass in the uncritical popular imagination that is unable to see and differentiate between the variety of films on offer. Edward Johnson, although more concerned with the art of Indian film posters, captures well the contemptuous attitudes towards Bollywood and other popular commercial Indian films as he writes:

Indian cinema has a reputation in the West founded more on myth than reality. 'Art' directors such as Satyajit Ray are given fulsome praise whilst the majority 'commercial' cinema receives nothing but ridicule and the entire industry is pilloried as specious dross by people who then often confess to never having seen any of the films in question (Johnson 1987: 2).

Contrary to such common assertion, Bollywood comprises several genres of films, each with a dynamic of its own. A number of Indian film commentators have outlined the different genres of Bollywood films (see, for example, Garga 1996; Johnson 1987; Gokulsing and Dissanayake 1998; Ramachandran 1985; Rangoonwalla 1982; Vasudev and Lenglet 1983). Edward Johnson (1987), in particular, offers a useful introductory taxonomy of Bollywood films. According to Johnson five generic strands of films can be loosely identified. Devotional Films, Historical Films, Social Films or Topicals, Muslim Social Films, and Masala Films. Moti Gokulsing and Wimal Dissanayake (1998) describe a sixth genre, that of Romantic Films (see Appendix). At a basic level of description a familiar feature of Bollywood movies is their recurrent themes of boy-meets-girl love story, and binary oppositions in the representation of East and West, tradition and modernity, rich and poor, the village and the city, and so forth. However, as is discussed in the reading of the film *Pardes* (Foreign Land, dir. Subhash Ghai, 1997) in Chapter 3, such themes are actively challenged by Bollywood viewers and with the emergence of the diaspora as an important export market for the films since the nineties, film-makers are rethinking their approaches to established conventions and genres in the light of contemporary audience expectations.

It is important to note that Bollywood movies are not indiscriminately viewed. Of the 200 annual films made, only 20 per cent, at the very best go on to be successful at the box office in India (i.e., manage to recuperate back their initial investment plus some profits), and only one or two become real blockbusters in terms of popularity with audiences and incredible profits. This 20:80 ratio of successes over failures has continued for at least two decades now (Chopra 1997a; Katiyar 1994). Evidently, the bulk of Bollywood films are not easily accepted by Indian audiences. Neither top stars, nor film music, nor storyline can guarantee box office success. The ability of being able to appropriately assess the 'mood' and expectations of film audiences is a skill only few film-makers have.

Furthermore, the movies that flop or make it big in India may perform quite differently in box offices across planet Bollywood. For example, the 1998 film *Dil Se...* (From The Heart), a love story between an All India Radio reporter (Shahrukh Khan) and an Assamese freedom fighter (Manisha Koirala) directed by south Indian director Mani Ratnam, became the first-ever officially recorded Bollywood box-office success in the UK, attracting national and international media attention as a result (Chaudhary 1998; Goldenberg and Dodd 1998; Joshi 1998). It earned a remarkable £66,000 from just eight screens after two weeks of release. Ratnam's film grossed only £10,000 less than *The Avengers* (dir. Jeremiah S. Chechik, 1998, starring Sean Connery and Uma Thurman), from 152 fewer screens (*Empire* magazine, November 1998: 18). Since the success of *Dil Se...* the film magazine *Screen International* now features the ranking of box-office positions of the latest Bollywood movies alongside mainstream Hollywood ones that make it into the top 10 box-office listings in the UK. Interestingly, *Dil Se...* failed at the box office in India. The film's overt political agenda of the trials of the Assamese people on the India–China border, interwoven with a love story on the eve of India's 50 years of Independence celebrations, was said to have proved too much for Indian audiences. In contrast, Bollywood-goers in Britain were reported to have acclaimed the film's handling of an original politicised plot through a populist convention, and the fact that current heart-throb Shahrukh Khan was playing the lead, coupled with A.R. Rehman's pulsating music score meant that *Dil Se...* became a 'must see movie' in the UK well ahead of its release (see Joshi 1998). In fact, for the first two months after its release in September *Dil Se...* was shown on five screens, five times per day, at staggered intervals at the 14-screen Cineworld complex in Feltham, west London. Each show was a complete sellout as an average of 3,000 spectators per day watched the film in this one cinema alone (Chaudhary 1998).

Bollywood vs. Hollywood

The exact origins of the formation of the term 'Bollywood' are unknown but as Satvinder Rana, BBC Radio Derby (UK) presenter of the *Aaj Kal* (Today Tomorrow) show and columnist for Birmingham's *Spice* magazine in the summer of 1996, speculates:

> I'm not sure why it [Bollywood] has become such an acceptably standard word in our language, especially since it was probably conjured up by some cocky white journalist to describe the Indian film industry in a somewhat idiosyncratic and derogatory manner.

Uncertainties aside, however, Bollywood is more popularly described in relation to, and against, the hegemony of Hollywood. As an album sleeve for a compilation tape of contemporary Bollywood film songs announced on the front cover of *Cineblitz* magazine (Summer 1997),

'Bollywood vs. Hollywood'. The naming and popular usage of the Mumbai film industry as 'Bollywood' not only reveals on a literal level an obvious reworking of the appellation of the cinema of Hollywood, but, on a more significant level, that Bollywood is able to serve alternative cultural and social representations away from dominant white ethnocentric audio-visual possibilities.

In qualitative interviews that I conducted with audiences of Bollywood films and popular culture in Birmingham, UK, respondents pointed out that they had social investments in Bollywood media as for them it articulated an affirmation of their eclectic British–South Asian cultural identity (Dudrah 2002a). A common talking point that came up in the interviews was that there was an issue of representation at stake in seeing Indian film stars relating to a South Asian imaginary that conveyed on-screen pleasures for South Asian audiences in complex and varied ways across different film genres and played out by different actors and actresses. Representations that depict a myriad sense of South Asianness are actively sought, particularly given the limited range of images depicting South Asians in the mainstream mass media in the West (see also Shakur and D'Souza 2003).

Furthermore, outside the film capital of Mumbai, Bollywood is also one signifier, among many others, of the wider Indian film industry as the largest in the world.[6] The total production of films from India is calculated at about 900 annual films (Kasbekar 1996), and in monetary terms it is second only to Hollywood. On a Birmingham (UK) Asian radio show it was announced that throughout India's 800 cinemas, 10 million official ticket sales are exchanged daily, and 5 billion annual visits are made to the theatres (four times as many than in the USA) generating an estimated income, in the region, of £500 million. Furthermore, India's combined cinema industries employ over 500,000 full-time workers (BBC Asian Network 1997).[7] These figures make for an interesting comparison to those of film-going in the West where the sporadic make up of cinema audiences, growth in leisure services, advent of non-terrestrial television, video and DVD rental sales, and proliferation of home-based entertainment technology has seen a decline in cinema attendances. In Britain, for example, annual cinema attendance figures in 1999 were recorded at a maximum high of 139.5 million, having risen from a low of 54 million attendances in 1984. Even then, the high of 139.5 million visits to UK cinemas in 1999 is slightly higher than cinema attendance figures in 1979, illustrating not so much an increase in the activity of cinema going but a moderate return to watching predominantly Hollywood movies on the big screen (see Murphy 2000).[8] In comparison, in spite of the modernisation and increase in leisure pursuits in urban South Asian societies cinema going remains, at present, much more of a public event to people in India than in the West (see Breckenridge 1995).

The list of aforementioned examples help to briefly illustrate the scope, size and appeal of the Bollywood cultural phenomenon, and to indicate potential areas for further research which would require careful examination. This would involve taking into account, amongst other issues, questions of film as an economic and cultural industry,[9] high culture versus mass culture debates, culturally specific notions of aesthetics and audience preferences, and the role of popular forms in responding to and engaging with global cultural identities. What this book aims to do through select areas of analysis is to elaborate on an interdisciplinary dialogue between sociology, film, media and cultural studies as compatible and appropriate fields of subject enquiry to illuminate some of the social and cultural possibilities that are rendered through the global workings of Bollywood cinema as a film and media industry that seeks to popularise its films for maximum economic profit and in turn is entered into an unpredictable relationship amongst its audiences. The methodological imperative for taking up select areas of Bollywood cinema for socio-cultural consideration and aesthetic analysis across interdisciplinary boundaries operates through the following organising frameworks that enable this book to set out its project of a sociological dialogue with studies of the cinema. The organising frameworks are: the relationship between Bollywood and its South Asian diasporas; the performance of social identity in Bollywood cinema; Bollywood cinema as a cinematic assemblage; and, the possible futures of and beyond Bollywood cinema.

NOTES TOWARDS A METHODOLOGY: DOING SOCIOLOGICAL AND FILM RESEARCH TOGETHER

Methodologically, this book operates at the intersection of research analyses and frameworks across sociology, film and media, and cultural studies as a dialogue towards exploring the workings of a media phenomenon, that of Bollywood cinema, as it mediates and functions socially across some of the aspects of its production through to its life as a cinematic screen text—i.e., the film—through to its articulation as a wider popular cultural form that is used by its audiences in varying ways.

Select films are used throughout the book for analysis and elaboration that have proved popular at and beyond their initial box-office release amongst Indian and diasporic South Asian audiences over the years. Where possible key films have been chosen that are readily available not only on video but also on DVD where the option of viewing the film in a number of subtitled languages, not least in English, is available, thereby allowing readers of this book to cross reference and make their own minds up about the analyses of the individual films that are offered throughout.

The kinds of cross-disciplinary analysis that are taken up in this book include not just formal and aesthetic analyses of the film texts (a traditional concern of film studies) but also to think further about Bollywood popular culture beyond the film texts through to its cultures of songs and music, cinema going, Bollywood dance clubs in the diaspora (predominantly the focus is on Bollywood cinema's translation at a queer club night), and the mainstream Western interaction with Bollywood films and popular culture. A focus on these latter kinds of textual examples is firmly located within cultural and social theoretical discourses of social interaction, cultures of production and social meaning-making, as well as examining the intersection of representation and social power relationships in the film texts themselves, to the social possibilities that are interpreted by audiences. This latter and simultaneous focus, then, derives much from the tools and methods of sociology, film and media, and cultural studies that are brought together to initiate and actualise the dialogue across these different and related subject disciplines. Thus, *Sociology Goes to the Movies* advocates and illustrates ways in drawing together methods such as participant observation, the use of qualitative extended interviews (on the use of these methods as applied in media settings, see Jensen 2002; Schroder et al. 2003), alongside the textual analysis of films and film cultures (Bordwell and Thompson 2001; Cook 1999; Hayward 2000; Monaco 2000).[10] In this way aesthetic analysis is articulated with socio-cultural commentary and critique to offer a flexible and idiosyncratic sociology of Bollywood cinema:

one that uses cinematic and popular cultural sources qualitatively to read culture and society.

Bollywood and the South Asian Diaspora

The Indian and South Asian diaspora more generally is now almost always an important consideration in the production, distribution, anticipated monetary returns and potential audience reach for Bollywood cinema, especially where films are centred on urban settings or characters. The Indian diaspora alone has been conservatively estimated at 11 million people around the world and is considered as one of the fastest growing global diasporic communities (see Mishra 2002: 235–41).[11] Of late, the diaspora's prominence becomes apparent not only at the level of diegetic activity in Hindi cinema but also in terms of creative collaboration. Cultural producers from the South Asian diaspora are also making their input in Bollywood films through production possibilities. For example, the film *Hum Tum* (Me and You, dir. Kunal Kohli, 2004) features the musical and vocal talents of British Asian RandB fusion artists Rishi Rich with Veronica and Juggy D on a song of the music album, entitled *U n I*. This song accompanies the international travels of the two main urban Indian characters Karan (Saif Ali Khan) and Rhea (Rani Mukherjee) whilst their love story develops throughout the film across India, the Netherlands, New York and Paris.

U n I follows in the footsteps of earlier British South Asian and Indian collaborations in the production of Bollywood cinema. For instance, Birmingham based remix artist Bally Sagoo worked on the music soundtrack of *Kartoos* (Weapon, dir. Mahesh Bhatt, 1999), and almost two decades earlier the late British Asian singer Nazia Hassan playbacked on the soundtrack of the film *Qurbani* (Sacrifice, dir. Feroz Khan, 1980) to the eighties disco-style 'Aap jaise koi' (Someone Like You) track.

Diasporic South Asians who partake in the cultures of watching Bollywood films and their related popular cultural activities are also amalgamating and recreating Bollywood film cultures into their everyday social lives. By way of an example consider the following mobile text message that was sent to me by my 15-year-old cousin, who received it from one of her girlfriends at school:

Life brngz 'kabhi kushi kabhi ghum',
how long each lasts 'na tum jano na hum',
thru thick n thin 'hum saath saath hai',
no1 noz 'kal ho naa ho',
neva 4gt 'main hoon na' x

The message roughly translates into English as 'Life brings sometimes happiness and sometimes sadness, how long each lasts neither you know nor I, through thick and thin we are always together, no one knows whether there will be a tomorrow, never forget I'm here now, kiss.' This message was doing its rounds in a high school South Asian youth culture in London and was then sent on to me, as well as possibly to others around the country, and even abroad—my cousin tells me that she also sent it to our relatives in India. It draws on the titles of contemporary Bollywood films and songs and is written and recreated in the shorthand and eclectic language of text messaging and diasporic South Asian youth culture—the text is a hybrid of compacted and urban street slang with the vocabulary of Hinglish (spoken Bollywood film Hindi and English words articulated together). What is further interesting about this text message is its possible source—was it originally made up in India and then sent around the world via mobile phone technology, or was it created somewhere in the diaspora, in the UK or in the US for instance, before being circulated up and down the country and then on to other parts of the world?

Both examples of the text message and the film music productions between India and the UK, are indicative of the ways in which Bollywood films have become a part of the diasporic South Asian popular culture more generally and also of the alliances, collaborations and routes that are possible in the movement of this popular culture in globalisation.

However, the cultural fluidity of these two examples also sits alongside a critique of Bollywood cinema's relationship to the Indian diaspora. Whilst the diaspora is becoming a regular feature of contemporary Bollywood cinema, some commentators have criticised the representation and use of the diaspora in popular Hindi cinema as being limited by the nationalist and narrow concerns of its filmmakers (see, for example, Mankekar 1999; Mishra 2002: Chapter 8; Uberoi 1998). It has been argued that much of contemporary Bollywood cinema engages the diaspora diegetically in terms of a space of desire; a desire that is set in urban India and in the overseas space (especially in the West), of wealth and luxury accumulation that Bollywood cinema endorses. Furthermore, Mishra (2002: 245–47), by drawing on the work of Marie Gillespie on Hindi video film consumption amongst British Indian families in Southall, west London (Gillespie 1995), unfortunately goes on to repeat Gillespie's flawed claim that a generational split can be detected in the ways in which first and second generation diasporic South Asians read popular Hindi cinema—the former as purveyors of cultural tradition and the latter as struggling to come to terms with cultural negotiation between the two generations.[12] Mishra is therefore unable to suggest or demonstrate more detailed readings or complex uses of Bollywood film cultures by its diasporic audiences, and instead turns to cite the filmic works of Hanif Kureishi's *My Beautiful Laundrette* (1985) or Srinivas Krishna's *Masala* (1991) as more appropriate examples of reflexive engagements with the South Asian diaspora (see Mishra 2002: 241–44).

Counter to such readings, Chapter 3 in this book draws on qualitative interviews that were conducted in the city of Birmingham, UK, with young British South Asians who viewed Bollywood films as part of their cultural activities. In particular, readings of the film *Pardes*, a romantic blockbuster that deals with relationships between South Asia and the South Asian diaspora through the pursuit of love across India and America, are offered by my respondents and ultimately by myself, through the interpretations that I place upon their readings, as an invitation to consider further the possible ways in which Bollywood cinema represents the diaspora, and moreover how Bollywood cinema is itself read and understood by sections of the diaspora that actively partake as its audiences.

Throughout this book, then, the social processes of globalisation—the expansion of capital and capitalism, the compression of time and space, increased cultural commodification, the interactions between the local and the global, all increasingly occurring in and indicative of the late modern era (Harvey 1989; Jameson 1991; Sassen 1998)—and the social condition of the diaspora as an expression of the social, cultural and political dimensions of globalisation as setting into play a relationship between the homeland of ancestral origin and the new place of migratory settlement through actual and imagined social and cultural movements (Appadurai 1990; Dudrah 2004; Tololyan 1996) are elaborated on in this work. The engagement with sociological concerns of globalisation and the diaspora are deciphered through the textual representations that Bollywood cinema is able to offer of these processes aesthetically. Furthermore, these textual representations and their wider social meanings are interrogated further and complexified through the use of cultural and social methods such as qualitative interview research (Chapter 3) and participant observation (Chapters 4 and 5). How Bollywood cinema itself is an example of the socio-cultural flows and routes of globalisation is also taken up for comment and analysis in this book (Chapter 6).

The Performance of Identity

Perhaps one of the diverse yet complex ways in which cinema interacts with its audiences is through a relationship of familiarity and repetition. One is not thinking here of the familiarity or the repetition of film genres alone that draws audiences to particular kinds of film events and narratives (cf. Neale 2000: 9–29), but rather I am alluding here to the immediate way in which films translate a sense of our social selfhoods as refracted on the screen. The products of cinema—films—provide an immediate visual encoding of the human form on screen. This form is most often agile—it appears, it moves, it disappears and then re-appears again through the staged movements of the performers, as well as through edit cuts. The human form is further punctuated by, and given additional meaning through, the film's soundtrack, or through the absence of, or selective use of, sound and music. In this way, we get to see a body on screen represented as a stand-in, as a familiar presence that moves through repetition, as a character for the audience's possible identification.

This identification can work across a nexus of aesthetic and social relations that come together to offer an intended message of identification (of race, gender, class, and nation for example) that has been crafted together by the film's production team, where the director directs the actor/actress to perform, who in turn nuances a particular kind of action of that direction, that is captured in particular ways by the camera movement, lighting, post-production digital manipulation and so forth. These technical instances of the production process come together as the filmic text, that are mediated further by the audience's interaction with the intended messages. A kind of performance that purports to be like the audiences' everyday familiarity, or at the very least within the audiences' realm of comprehension, is set into play that aims to engage the audience through its characters, stories and messages as not too unlike them. How this performance, its very nature and its composition, sets about in using the human body, as it is captured by the technical equipment and translated in possibly numerous ways by different viewers, is the subject of the second part of Chapter 3. In particular, the second section of this chapter considers the performance of urban and diasporic Indian identity as it is enacted through the star body of actor Shahrukh Khan. In fact, as is suggested in Chapter 3, we need to be aware of the cultural and social capital of some actors/actresses over others; those who go on to become 'stars'; those who earn multi-million rupees, pounds and dollars through lucrative commercial deals and sponsorships that are a part of cinema's global distribution and circulation; and those who go on to create an affinity with their fans around the world. How certain stars are able to perform a particular kind of urban and diasporic Indian and South Asian identity, as telling of the ways of the embodiment of cultural globalisation in contemporary Bollywood cinema, is explored in the latter half of the chapter.

Bollywood Cinema as an Assemblage

Implicit in some of the more recent studies of Bollywood cinema is a notion of desire as operating in the films that offer its Indian and diasporic audiences an on-screen diegetic activity that addresses facets of their selfhood at the individual, nation state and/or transnational levels (see, for example, Chakravarty 1996 and Nandy 1998 on individual and nation state melodramatic trials and desires; and, Mishra 2002 on diasporic desire). Mishra's book in particular is subtitled 'Temples of Desire' referring to the complex, dream-like and psychoanalytical ways in which the films are said to encourage a relationship between audiences as viewers through which psycho-social dynamics are played out in the dark theatre auditoriums on the canvas of the cinema screens. However, what is missing from these contributions is a sense of how desire is actualised, and how it comes into being. In these studies, desire is also only considered as formulated at the moment of the audience's viewing of that which is represented on screen; they rarely take us beyond considerations of representations at the textual level. What is further unclear in these studies is whether desire can work outside of the immediate cinematic screen. Put another way, is desire only available in the viewing process, or is it also a part of, and connected to, other social and cultural processes? And, how might we usefully think of desire beyond textual representations alone?

In order to elaborate on the kinds of desires available in films and to consider how desire works in and through the popular cultures of Hindi cinema, this book considers Bollywood cinema as an assemblage. The term 'assemblage' is used throughout this book as implying a particular understanding about the production of desire. I am indebted, here, to John Rajchman's (1977) reading of Gilles Deleuze and Felix Guattari as offering an understanding of the processes involved in the production of desire through the coming together of cultural and social assemblages. In this view desire is considered as part of the formation of an effect, a sensation that is part of and articulated between actual and metaphoric bodies—the actual and metaphoric body of cinema as a cultural and entertainment industry interacting with the actual body of its audiences. Cinema can be likened to a metaphoric body as its audio-visual signs and codes signify a range of meanings (for example, race, gender, class, sexuality, the nation state, and so forth). It is also an actual body in terms of the functioning of its materiality (for example, capital, film production teams, cinematic technology and equipment, cinema houses, cinema's global networks of distribution and circulation, and so forth). The actual body of the cinematic audience is a physical and biological as well as a social and cultural construction that interacts with the body of cinema in terms of affects and sensations that produce particular kinds of desires (for example, around caste, race, class, gender, sexuality, and so on). These desires are partly in circulation in the immediate social and cultural worlds of the audience and are then mediated further through an interaction with the cinematic assemblage. In Chapter 4, the cinematic assemblages of the Eagle Theatre in the borough of Queens, and the Loews cinema in Time Square in New York City, are elaborated on and contrasted as criss-crossed by socio-cultural intensities, affects, flows, voltages and vibrations as part of an actual and metaphoric machine (i.e., cinema) that can be considered as a non-human body. The socio-cultural flows and affects of this body are effects (hence affect-effects) of a desiring-production, of energies, and materialities of force that enable the assemblage to enter into new connections, networks and articulations. In this way we are able to think of cinema, its filmic products, and their interaction with audiences in actual spaces as moving beyond the representational. This also allows us to consider further the connections and the workings of representation as part of a wider circuit of social, cultural and economic relations in the era of globalisation. Chapter 4 utilises participant observation alongside textual analysis to elaborate on and refine the theoretical developments in film studies (haptic codes in the cinematic experience, metaphors of the body and skin, and Indian rasa theory), urban sociology and cultural geography (the location of places and spaces as informing subjectivity formation), and in cultural studies (identity, representation and diaspora studies) to situate and offer an exploration of diasporic South Asian identity formation vis-à-vis Bollywood cinema going at these two sites in New York City.

Beyond Bollywood

An analysis of popular Hindi cinema through an interdisciplinary social and cultural lens would not be complete without considering how this assemblage is connected to, and quotes from, other cultural and social sources and referents. Bollywood draws from a range of references in the composition of its films and music ranging from South Asian religious texts, to historical folk tales, to other Asiatic cinemas; from regional South Asian musical genres and lyrics to Western pop and rock music. Perhaps Bollywood cinema's use of references from mainstream Hollywood cinema has caused the most concern. Bollywood cinema has been considered to be either an imitation of Hollywood films and storylines in popular journalism and in sections of academic criticism, or as more usefully borrowing these sources and reconfiguring them through its own sensibilities. Chapter 6 considers some of these criticisms levelled at Bollywood cinema and questions their purpose. The chapter goes on to consider the movement and growth of Bollywood cinema vis-à-vis the stage of international popular culture and entertainment through the use of Bollywood's hybrid aesthetics by diasporic South Asian film-makers and by mainstream Western film-makers too. How and in what ways is Bollywood used as a cultural reference and resource in these different constituencies of cultural production is taken up for comment and analysis. The increasing interest in Indian audiences and in Bollywood cinema by transnational corporate players from the American cinema industries, and also by non-resident Indian (NRI) venture capitalists is considered in terms of Bollywood cinema's arrival as a player in the global cultural commodity markets.[13]

These frameworks, then, set into play a methodology that is interested in the cultural and social dimensions of Bollywood cinema as a global film industry; one that operates as films and wider popular culture, that in turn are entered into unpredictable relationships with and made sense of by its audiences in varying ways. Thus, the chapters that follow offer the following: Chapter 2 introduces an important aspect of Bollywood films—songs and music. Together these are considered as a way into the cinema's eclectic aesthetic composition, into areas of its production process, and as a way into accessing some of the key thematic issues that recur throughout Bollywood cinema—the depiction of love and romance, and an engagement with tradition and modernity.

Chapter 3 offers an analysis of the film *Pardes* as read by diasporic British South Asian audiences by drawing on qualitative interview research. The chapter also offers a reading of the on-screen performances of urban Indian and diasporic identities through a case study of the actor Shahrukh Khan as a contemporary 'star' in Bollywood cinema's circulation amidst cultural globalisation. Taken together, these two sections consider the role and representations of urban India and the diaspora in recent Bollywood cinema.

Whereas in the previous chapters, the notion of the cinematic assemblage is touched upon and alluded to throughout their topics and analyses, Chapter 4 explicitly engages with the cinematic assemblages of two cinema houses in New York—the Eagle in Jackson Heights and the Loews in Times Square. Drawing primarily on participant observation methods and fieldwork notes to elaborate on and refine select cultural and social theory, this chapter sets into play a consideration of the actualisation of desire in the act of Bollywood cinema going across considerations from urban and cultural geography, diaspora and globalisation, and the textual representations of Bollywood films as partial scripts of local and global affects.

Chapter 5 offers a commentary and analysis of the redeployment of Bollywood's boy-meets-girl love stories and song and dance sequences in the urban diasporic space of the queer club night. The social analysis of Bollywood's queer audiences using the original Bollywood film texts and transforming them into new cultural translations and possibilities is set in context amidst the recent fascination of Bollywood popular culture by the mainstream Western entertainment and cultural industries. The way in which Bollywood songs, music and dance are reconfigured by queer audiences to interrogate the relationship between cultural politics in the homeland and in the diaspora is also highlighted.

Chapter 6 situates Bollywood cinema further within the context of globalisation both textually, in terms of the changes that are occurring in the aesthetics of the films as sources of cultural mimicry, and in operational terms through the increasing co-production possibilities that are taking shape between different players in its local and global industry. It also discusses how the aesthetics of Bollywood cinema is being redeployed by diasporic South Asian film-makers, as examples of global cultural production and film-making practice. The chapter offers a social commentary and critique about how the lives of diasporic South Asians has been depicted by this group of film-makers as well.

SINGING FOR INDIA: SONGS IN THE BOLLYWOOD FILM

In India life begins and ends with music. For instance, a newborn baby is greeted into the world by songs ... there is a song and dance when he weds and dies.

—Kalyanji, music director[1]

This chapter examines the development of Bollywood cinema as a cultural form which through its use of song and music spans both film and popular culture. It primarily explores the origins of song and music in Bollywood film and also examines the position of song and music vis-à-vis the movie's narrative and economy. In addition, this chapter explores both the stylistic features and the production processes of Bollywood films and also pays attention to a recurring theme within contemporary Bollywood cinema—of the negotiation of tradition and modernity. This is followed by a textual analysis of key musical moments in the film *Hum Aapke Hain Koun..!* (Who am I to you!, dir. Sooraj Barjatya, 1994), one of the most significant blockbusters of Bollywood cinema, and an ostensibly conservative love story which plays out tensions between tradition and modernity. The discussion of the film will move beyond the contribution of the film director to consider the collaborative input of music directors, musicians, playback artists and performers, to show that Bollywood film and music function in a symbiotic relationship markedly different from any Western cinematic model that establishes song, music and dance as central to the movie's aesthetic.

BOLLYWOOD: BEYOND THE MUSICAL

Song and dance are integral to the classic Bollywood movie, and with many Bollywood productions it is the songs that are first developed. But Indian popular films are not seen as musicals; they are not genre films at all in the Western sense of the word. Hindi cinema cannot be forced into Western film-making categories. In one Bollywood film it is possible to include all the Western film genres—musical, romantic, comedy, action, thriller, tragedy, and melodrama. These disparate modes of storytelling are bound together into a coherent whole by songs. According to Jane Feuer, writing on Hollywood musicals, they 'not only *showed* you singing and dancing, they were *about* singing and dancing' (Feuer 1993: x);[2] they are about Hollywood, and about entertainment. In contrast, Bollywood films use singing and dancing to *show* you the story.

Song and dance plays a more 'organic' role operating beyond the level of 'show business' spectacle to further the film's narrative, and to enrich it through metaphor. While spectacle is often about development, grandeur and modernity, Bollywood song and dance numbers complement this by playing an extra-narrative role of linking a film to Indian tradition, quoting classical performances,[3] or religious imagery. Bollywood films are about spectacle, but also about a fantasy of India. In a song sequence, a film's hero and heroine become more than the characters they play. They are first and foremost Bollywood stars, who, over time, become mythic figures for the development of passion between men and women.[4] Song sequences often directly provide a route back to the mythic discourses (of, for example, Ram and Sita, Shiva and Parvati, Radha and Krishna, or of Sufi and Christian traditions within South Asia) from which Indian art forms stem, so that stars become identified with mythic figures, and their story becomes a metaphor for another, even more deeply familiar, story.[5] In counterpoint to this depiction of 'traditional' India, Bollywood also increasingly represents a new middle-class India, one of affluence, technology and globalisation (see Dwyer 2000); an India represented alongside the traditional one in the film *Hum Aapke Hain Koun..!*, as is discussed later.

Since the first talkie *Alam Ara* (dir. Ardeshir Irani, 1931)—a form that was a direct transfer from Parsi Theatre—Bollywood films have been structured around a core of six to eight songs (or even once, so legend has it, 71).[6] In fact, classical Indian theatre has for some 2,000 years considered '*sangeeta*—that is, song, instrumental music and dance—to be an essential feature of the dramatic performance' (Kasbekar 1996: 369). The success of *Alam Ara* and its songs set a trend that the Indian film industry has followed ever since.

There is a different aesthetic tradition at the root of Bollywood, that critic Ravi Vasudevan traces back to the 'frontal' style of classic Indian painting and performing arts that 'goes against Western laws of perspective in their lack of depth and stylistic emphasis on surface' (Vasudevan 1989: 33). Bollywood can be regarded as superficiality without considering that this is produced by an entirely different set of cinematic priorities.[7]

Popular Hindi films are often referred to as 'masala' movies, because a good movie 'blends the masalas in proper proportions' (Thomas 1985: 124), expertly mixing an ordered succession of modes, from comedy, to romance, to melodrama. The very swiftness of the transition from one form to another, that to a Western eye may seem improbable, is a mark of a film-maker's skill, of including something for everybody while maintaining the film's balance. Perhaps the only Western analogy for such an omnibus form is Elizabethan drama, as seen in Shakespearean plays.

It is the very predictability of the Bollywood narrative that provides its pleasure, with the strength and reassuring familiarity of the narrative provoking anticipation not of *what* will happen next, but of *how* it will happen (ibid.: 130). And as for the songs, there is no need, in a cinema that prioritises emotional engagement over 'realism', to justify their inclusion through such elaborate devices as a show within a film, as is done in Hollywood backstage musicals. They are, instead, so tightly integrated within the flow of the film that 'if you miss a song, you have missed an important link between one part of the narration and the next' (director Raj Kapoor as quoted in ibid.: 127). The Bollywood musical numbers can operate *both* at the levels of narrative and spectacle.

Grand settings and glittering costumes may have little to do with the actual plot, except represent the scale of the hero and heroine's love, but this does not diminish their importance as one of the central attractions of Bollywood cinema. Traditional Indian aesthetic conventions have always placed great importance on spectacular visual displays—using elaborate masks or stylised make-up—and film enables these displays to take on more ambitious proportions. In *Mughal-e-Azam* (The King of Azam, dir. K. Asif, 1960), a sumptuous historical tale of a prince and a slave girl, one of the crucial moments of the film is a song and dance number performed in a specially constructed hall of mirrors so that the dancing slave girl is reflected in every mirror in the hall. The first scene shot in Technicolor in an Indian film, it was inserted into the middle of a black and white movie. Such is the repeat attraction of this film for Bollywood audiences that it is has undergone a complete digital colour and sound overhaul in 2004 and has been re-released for national and international Bollywood audiences.[8]

Song sequences can also operate on a metaphorical level, enabling a step *beyond* the story. They can be dream sequences, sometimes stated, sometimes implied; they are often fantasies for the protagonists as well as the audience. And, on a metaphorical level, songs allow ideological exposition outside the narrative, turning subtext into text around themes such as tradition versus Westernisation, with songs acting as 'a bridge between tradition and modernity' (Kasbekar 1996: 372). For example, in the film *Main Khiladi Tu Anari* (I'm the Player, You're the Amateur, dir. Sameer Malkan, 1994) the song 'Chura ke dil mera' ('Stealing my Heart') brings together the protagonists—a Mumbai policeman and his demure companion (Akshay Kumar and Shilpa Shetty)—in a mutual declaration of love enacted entirely outside of the world of their experience. They are transported to a deserted tropical beach and an opposition between nature and culture is constructed. The setting moves towards civilisation as the bay fills with boats and then becomes a building site with hero and heroine relocating to a luxury yacht where they perform an energetic and sexualised dance, the heroine clad in Western-style leopard-skin leggings. The development process is then reversed, back to the construction site, then to a beach hut at night, through an aisle of trees, a cornfield, and, finally, a coconut grove. Sitting on the beach by a fire, the hero plays a violin, but then stops to grab the heroine by the hair and pulls her towards him in a passionate manner. The sequence ends with an aerial shot of the woman lying alone on a vast, empty beach: she has dreamt the whole song.

From this song sequence we learn that the beach utopia was a fantasy; the heroine has never left Mumbai. In fact, the protagonists are not even shown together; the policeman has been tricked into asking the woman to marry him over the phone (the song beings after Shilpa Shetty telephones Akshay Kumar at his police station and teases him in a sexual, playful manner). This song is the only evidence that they share a genuine mutual passion and is therefore central to the narrative, while at the same time taking an enormous diversion from it. The protagonists' romance, through the song as dream sequence, is played out against a backdrop of an urbanised India undergoing modernisation and development, and these are key motifs within which the love story is often negotiated in contemporary Indian cinema. Not only is this a dream about being with a lover, it is also a dream about affluence and access to middle-class India for both, the protagonists and the audience; an audience consisting predominantly of the working sectors of society. Yet, alongside the aspirational fantasies of this middle-class utopia runs a critique of the process of modernisation. Increasing affluence and access to a 'Westernised' commodity culture is acceptable only alongside the retention of 'traditional' Indian culture and values. Thus songs carry the weight of an extra-narrative debate about constructed versions of India, in addition to acting as narrative accelerators.

Behind the Scenes: The Bollywood Production Process

The Bollywood song and dance numbers lie at the heart of Bollywood films, both stylistically and economically. It is believed that good songs make good movies, and the songs come first in the production process. Music directors are given only the broad outline of a film— the main stars and a story outline—on which to work (Marre and Charlton 1985: 142). They write and record at least six songs for the movie with 'playback singers', many of whom have achieved the same high celebrity status as the movie stars who act and mime to their voices. Lata Mangeshkar is one playback singer who has helped shape the sound of Indian popular music, with half a century of recording and 25,000 songs to her credit (Kasbekar 1996: 370).

Music directors draw on a range of musical traditions and styles for their songs, from Indian classical and folk music, to, and increasingly so, Western pop. This acts as a bridge between signifiers of tradition and modernity, so that Western and traditional instruments are combined. Furthermore, recognisable popular melodies are borrowed so that an audience may find themselves reminded of George Michael's 'Faith', or Michael Jackson's 'Thriller', in the middle of a film song. Indian musical director Kalyanji describes his music as a synthesis inspired from every source. He views Indian film music as a form at once sophisticated—'I feel that we are definitely ahead of other countries in music'—and simple—'we try to write songs so simple that they can be hummed by everybody. Every song should be as simple as a nursery rhyme. This is where our art as music directors lies' (Marre and Charlton 1985: 141–42). At its best, this hybrid yet simple musical form of the Bollywood song can bypass the barriers of caste, age and region to become a hit with broad appeal.

The film director shoots the 'song picturisations', with the stars miming and dancing to a playback recording of the songs. These pictuarisations involve high production values—supporting dancers, grandiose sets and foreign locations. The completed song picturisations are then shown to financiers to persuade them to invest further in the film and only then is the money raised to film the remaining segments between the songs. If this process seems unorthodox by Western standards, its logic is deeply rooted in the Indian tradition of popular theatre where only the song and dance numbers are composed and rehearsed, with the dialogue and witty repartee, in-between, improvised at the point of performance (Kasbekar 1996: 369).

Much of this history of the Bollywood production process is beginning to change, but with songs still as a core feature. Until the late nineties, scriptwriters often had little notice to prepare a scene's dialogue for shooting. Production on the rest of the film was sporadic, taking anything from six months to three years, as 'dates' had to be booked with the stars (Gokulsing and Dissanayake 1998: 102), who may have been working on as many as 20 films at once, and regularly shooting scenes for two or three different films on the same day. However, with the professionalisation of the film industry by a new generation of directors, producers and scriptwriters who prepare their material and dates in advance, and also the contemporary actors and actresses who are being selective about their roles and only doing one or two films at a time, the working context in the Bollywood film industry is fast changing (see Bamzai 2003; *India Today* 2004; see also Chapter 6).

While the movie is still in production, song picturisations are shown on television and in cinemas as pre-publicity for the film and its soundtrack. This demonstrates how Bollywood has hit upon a winning formula for combining contemporary music and the screen industries. Popular television programmes screen compilations of film song picturisations, and, moreover, the films themselves operate as a collection of songs for an audience for whom the cinema is their main source of popular music.[9] The soundtrack is either released six months before the film or even a year before a major production, and creates the 'buzz' that can determine whether or not a film is successful. However, music sales themselves do not fund films; piracy and illegal trading is too widespread, and the largest profits for producers comes from cinema admissions and video and disc sales or rentals. However, with film music making up 80 per cent of music sales in India (Marre and Charlton 1985: 141), it has become a dominant popular music form. Also, with film music promoting and selling the movies both the music and film industries enjoy a symbiotic relationship.

When a film is released, it is released in the cultural capital of Mumbai and also simultaneously across all Indian 'territories' and foreign and diasporic markets, including Britain, the United States, Australia and the Middle East. Only 20 per cent of films that go into production make it this far (ibid.: 143) and one in five films released is moderately successful. Hindi film audiences are fickle; they can either flock to a film or leave the auditorium empty on a whim that no Bollywood formula seems able to predict.

READING *HUM AAPKE HAIN KOUN..!*: FOURTEEN SONGS, TWO WEDDINGS AND A FUNERAL

Bollywood works by its own rules to which the critical model of the classic Hollywood musical cannot be easily applied. But perhaps

Jane Feuer's analysis of the musical in *The Hollywood Musical* (1993) can be reformulated for Bollywood, just as Bollywood reformulates Hollywood film plots in its own image. Feuer locates the musical's utopian vision in community, and Hindi screenwriter K.K. Shukla places kinship at the heart of Bollywood—'kinship emotion in India is very strong—so this element always works' (as quoted in Thomas 1985: 126). The vision of community for Bollywood has an explicit political root, in an ideal of a united India, originally promoted by then Prime Minister Nehru's policies in the immediate post-Partition era, which advocated the use of the 'All-India' film to counteract alienation between India's middle and working classes.[10] Social alienation is particularly pertinent to India as a developing country and films address this through their negotiation of tradition and modernity.

Signifiers of this antinomy include, for example, the role of men and women in relation to contemporary India. The tradition/modernity antinomy is often played out on the bodies of the film protagonists. Historically, in the 'masala' movie, the male action hero literally battled against the excesses of modernisation as he combated Westernised, capitalist villains. In romance, the hero had to choose between two models of femininity: the Westernised vamp or the virtuous virgin. The stark contrast was often visually signalled through the women's dress code and behaviour—one in Western dress while the other in traditional sari or salwar kameez. More recently, the playing out of these binaries has become much more fluid and complex. As India embraces modernity and becomes increasingly globalised, its film characters—both men and women—through costumes, aural and visual codes, and their performances are also meandering the tradition/modernity antinomy in changing ways (as is discussed later in relation to the representation of diaspora in Chapter 3).

The tradition/modernity opposition can be explored through a reading of the film *Hum Aapke Hain Koun..!*[11] This is not a typical masala movie in that it contains no violence, nor does it leap from one fantasy location to another. Instead, it tells its story primarily within a real world experienced by the characters and is better understood as a romance combined with various aspects of family melodrama. This chapter will pay attention to some aspects of the film's aural and visual style as created through the collaborative input of the film's music directors, playback singers and leading stars. The chapter qualitatively reads these sources from the film to comment on aspects of cultural and social change that are given meaning through this film.

HAHK, released in Mumbai on 5 August 1994, has been one of the most successful Indian films of all time. The box-office takings of the film in India were so high that it was not released on video until 1998. As *Movie International* commented on its popularity in India:

> Unless you live in a parallel universe, you cannot be unaware of the HAHK hysteria that hit India. Although this pop pastry slathered with frosting is a qualified triumph (easy-going but no depth), it sent the country into a diabetic frenzy that has resulted in unheard of queues even in the film's 26th week![12]

At cinemas in Mumbai, Pune and Hyderabad it sustained a box-office run in excess of 100 weeks. In Britain, *HAHK* was one of the first films that heralded a mid-nineties new wave of Bollywood cinema going. This was a few years before *Screen International* began to list Bollywood ticket returns across the UK and North America, which they started to do only in 1998 after the box-office impact of the film *Dil Se* (From the Heart, dir. Mai Ratnam, 1998). This film proved more popular than some of the Hollywood movies released at the same time.[13] At one London cinema, the Bellevue in Edgware, *HAHK* achieved a 52-week run. Factors such as the high quality of production, family values and no violence were cited by numerous Indian film commentators as contributing to its huge success.[14] In fact, such was the popularity of *HAHK* in Britain that it was adapted for BBC Radio by Kristine Landon-Smith, and then later for the stage by the Tamasha Theatre Company who titled it *Fourteen Songs, Two Weddings, and a Funeral*. The theatre production toured the UK in the winter of 1998.

HAHK can be described as a north Indian Hindu fantasy, centred on an extended, upper middle-class family, which functions perfectly as a loving community; a vision which is essentially conservative.[15] The film's events are traditional religious and family festivals revolving around marriage, birth and death, and the protagonists are prepared to sacrifice individual happiness for communal good, never rebelling against their situation or finding it repressive. In this way, the film can be read as a preferred version of Indian family life.

However, this is not to suggest that audiences everywhere accept the conservatism depicted in the movie unproblematically. In fact, the film has been openly acknowledged as an aspirational fantasy rather than a realistic portrayal of actual lived experience by audiences.[16]

HAHK is remarkable in that it contains 14 songs, significantly more than the average five or six for a Bollywood film, which relates perhaps to the prioritising of the representation of community over plot in the film as a whole. In fact, the film's plot is kept simple, by developing the love of the two central protagonists Prem and Nisha through a catalogue of family festivities and trials. Unlike other Bollywood formula storylines (rich boy meets poor girl, or vice versa), in HAHK the protagonists are of a similarly affluent class background, so that their social position is never challenged, lessening the potential transgression of their romance. In this sense the film remains essentially conservative. Furthermore, the presence of modern consumer goods in the background of the mise en scène (computers, mobile phones, VCRs), is used to illustrate the fact that while the characters are comfortable using modern technology they adhere to a 'traditional' Indian extended family lifestyle, and that joining in communal singing, dancing, sitting, eating, and praying together as a family unit is given priority. The moral universe is more emphasised than the consumer universe. Characters are deliberately set up to conform to or pose a threat to the moral order, so that one of the women competing for Prem's affections is depicted as too Westernised in dress and behaviour, while Nisha, in contrast, lives comfortably in both modern urban India and the 'traditional' Indian home, setting her up as the ideal candidate for marriage.

HAHK opens with a song, sung on screen by Prem and Nisha, as the film's credits roll. The opening song named after the title of the film, sets into motion the dilemma of the love story, 'Who Am I to You?', which is answered at the end of the film by the two characters replying Hum Aapke Hain (I am yours). The song is an antiphonal ballad in which the two characters are mesmerised by their newfound love for one another. The picturisation of the song is filmed in black and white, depicting a photograph coming to life. The movie's stills photographer was Gautam Rajadhyaksha, one of India's most successful photographers of film stars, and he captures the radiance and innocence of the two characters as they contemplate their first love. The face of each character fills half of the screen as they call and respond to each other, but they never share the same frame. Moreover, until the characters are introduced in the story as Prem and Nisha the viewer has no inkling of their identity as characters but sees them only as stars unfolding an emotional story which could be about the viewers themselves. The audience would immediately recognise the male and female leads, film stars Salman Khan and Madhuri Dixit, even before their names appear in the title credits. Popular Bollywood actors in India are accorded a larger than life status akin to demi-gods and godesses. The characters, Prem and Nisha, are affirmed this status through their shimmering white auras which are set against the black screen background depicting them as part divine and part human.

HAHK is an enthralling film primarily because of its songs, music and dancing which aim to seduce the viewers and involve them in the festivities and trials of the on-screen family. The importance of music and songs in the film can be gauged by the fact that its music director (in this case Raam Laxman) is given equal billing alongside the producers and directors on the film's publicity stills. Lata Mangeshkar and S.P. Balasubramanyam, two of India's most re-nowned singers, sing the title song, with lyrics by Dev Kohli.[17] The film's playback singers include seven of India's most sought after artists, each of whom brings a unique style of intonation and vocal representation to the film's large cast of 14 characters, spread across two families and two generations. With a multitude of actors and actresses, all playbacked by an impressive line up of singers, HAHK uses its songs, accompanying music and dancing to develop a storyline and create a film spectacle that is clearly appealing.

The second song of the film 'Wah wah Ram ji' (Ode to Lord Ram) is sung at a pilgrimage site where the two families meet to arrange the marriage of Prem's older brother Rajesh (Mohnish Behl) with Nisha's elder sister Pooja (Renuka Shahane). The song simulta-neously stages the rituals of pilgrimage through prayer and devotion to the idols of Ram, Sita and Laxman from the Ramayana; the performance of the engagement ceremony of Rajesh and Pooja; and the development of the attraction between Prem and Nisha. The temple is transformed from a site of pilgrimage to an extension of the family home as the two households join together in celebration. The anonymous pilgrims in the background join in the singing and dancing and thereby become extended family members. The pilgrims act as extra-diegetic signifiers for the audience and through their presence the actual audience is also invited to participate in the festivities. The music incorporates upbeat tablas and *dholak*s (drums), *shehnai*s (flute pipes) and sitars which are arranged to shift between temple music and tunes familiar at an Indian marriage. Here, the music acts as a narrative bridge between the religious and secular worlds. Prem and Nisha sing the verses which introduce their various siblings, while through the dances (choreographed by Jay Borade) they also play with and tease one another through facial and bodily gestures loosely taken from the dancing out of the mudras (Indian classical dance) (see Figure 2.1). This is reminiscent of stories from the Ramayana and Mahabharata wherein the playfulness of divine figures such as Ram and Sita or Radha and Krishna is considered as an exposition of their divine love for each other.

Figure 2.1: Nisha (Madhuri Dixit) and Prem (Salman Khan) tease one another in the song 'Wah wah Ram ji' in *HAHK*

As with the other songs in *HAHK*, tracks four and five in the film also help develop the love story of Prem and Nisha in addition to acting out the rituals of an Indian wedding. The fourth song 'Joote dedo, paise lelo' (Give the shoes, take the money) playbacked by Lata Mangeshkar, S.P. Balasubramanyam and a chorus, to the lyrics of Ravinder Rawal, vocalises the highly entertaining stand-off between the bride's sisters and the bridegroom's brothers. The bride's cohorts have, according to custom, stolen the bridegroom's shoes and will bargain for the highest monetary price from him for their return. It is the job of the groom's brothers to attempt to get them back. Prem and Nisha, with their gang of followers, are once again seen to tease and play with each other whilst acting and dancing out this highly popular ritual. The ritual is made all the more visually appealing as both sides are adorned in their best attire as they are at Rajesh and Pooja's wedding. Nisha stands out as the bride's sister in a stunning green and white *lengha* (fitted green blouse and dupatta, with flowing white skirt).[18] Although all present at the wedding are visually signalled as individuals through their different dress codes and costume colours, what matters more is their coming together as a social unit to act out the wedding through its varied modes of celebration. The song also makes use of the spacious layout of Nisha's parents' house, of the large dancehall in which numerous moving bodies, colours and dresses mingle together in a visual spectacle. Both boys and girls dance alongside and challenge each other as bickering couples: one asking for the shoes, the other for the money—'Joote dedo, paise lelo' (see Figure 2.2). As the song reaches its climax Nisha is in possession of the shoes and is being

Figure 2.2: Boys versus the girls: Prem and Nisha play–fight to obtain the groom's shoes whilst singing and dancing 'Joote dedo, paise lelo' in *HAHK*

chased by Prem in a final attempt to get them back. They run upstairs and enter a bedroom out of the sight of all the family members, falling on top of each other onto a bed. The song and music pauses momentarily. As they help each other up, Prem holds Nisha's arm and twists it towards him, signalling a romantic and sexual acceptance between the two. The music of the song begins again, capturing the importance and intimacy of this moment. Prem allows Nisha to run back to the families with the shoes. The girls sing and dance announcing to all that they are the winners. Prem stands on the balcony accepting defeat in the shoe game but triumphantly looks towards Nisha knowing that he has won her affection.

Despite this scene's root in traditional popular custom, there remains a tension between tradition and modernity within it. Couched within the timeworn and instantly recognised ritual, is a transgressive moment when the hero and heroine cross customary boundaries to make intimate physical contact. This moment embodies a tension at the heart of the film; the story is conservative, yet for the protagonists' love to begin, rules must be broken. From then on, whilst Prem and Nisha never overtly challenge the conservative status quo, the couple use traditional public rituals to mask and to facilitate their private courtship, so that the shared middle-class culture remains the dominant paradigm but is problematised as the protagonists manoeuvre within it to develop their love relationship.

No sooner has the 'Joote dedo, paise lelo' number finished than another song begins—'Saajan ke ghar' (House of my beloved)—which bids farewell in a melodramatic mode to Pooja from her parent's home and signals her new life with her husband and his family. In stark contrast to the playfulness and energy of the previous song this melody is more sad and slow in tempo, signalling a shift in focus from Prem and Nisha, to Rajesh and Pooja, and also in the rituals and customs of the wedding. In this way, and throughout *HAHK*, the songs and music move the film's narrative forward, and the key emotional moments of life are told through song and music.

OTHER INDIAS

The middle-class paradigm as seen in *HAHK* is not the only one in Bollywood cinema. If Bollywood films, through their songs and music, ostensibly encapsulate a middle-class utopian fantasy, then equally, from varied film-makers and across different categories of films, they also attract and attempt to represent the panoply of social existence that comprises India, not least other social classes and minorities. In this respect, let us briefly consider a couple of recent examples through Hindi film songs.[19]

Fiza (Winds of Change/Name of leading character of the film, dir. Khalid Mohammed, 2000) is a Muslim social drama of a struggling working-class family. The protagonist Fiza (Karisma Kapoor) searches for her brother Amaan (Hrithik Roshan) who disappears on the night of Hindu–Muslim riots in Mumbai and goes on to become a 'terrorist'. The first half of the film is structured through the memory flashbacks of other characters in the narrative as they remember Amaan.

In one recollection, Fiza's neighbour and mother both recall Amaan's love relationship with Shehnaz (Neha). During this flashback the song 'Aaja Mahiya' (Come my love), playbacked by Udit Narayan and Alka Yagnik, depicts Amaan and Shenaz's desire for each other. This song is picturised in the everyday diegetic setting of their world: lower- and working-class urban Mumbai street culture. Amaan and Shehnaz declare and announce their love for each other on the streets. We see them on the rooftops of apartments above the city; with fishermen and women in the docks who also accompany them as supporting dancers; with street kids and a food stall owner. The stall owner's coloured lunch box tops can be read within the mise en scène as offering different shades of love to Amaan and Shehnaz's relationship in the metropolis. They move on to a theatre space where they playact in Western attire which takes them above and beyond their usual working-class costumes, and then back on to the streets of Mumbai where Amaan literally dances in the middle of a busy road. They then dance above the road on a platform beside a large street hoarding advertising a well-known global toothpaste brand (possibly one of the film's co-financiers), to a canal side where city women are washing clothes and the open and flowing saris are used to lend the song a romantic mood and lush colours. The song ends on an upbeat tempo (see Figure 2.3). The ensuing scene is one of the present where Amaan's mother and neighbour sit in discomforting silence and anticipation of his return. The song 'Aaja Mahiya', then, works to develop an added human dimension to Amaan's character, but also in the wider narrative context of the film. The song situates the representational possibilities of its Muslim characters as everyday cultural citizens of the city, but against the backdrop of the tensions around the hegemonic and, at times, coercive Hindu state relations.

Figure 2.3: Amaan (Hrithik Roshan) and Shehnaz (Neha) dance with street kids, and literally above the street as everyday cultural citizens in the film *Fiza*

In another example, from the film *Chalte Chalte* (Along the Way, dir. Aziz Mizra, 2003), the cityscape is again used as the background through which the love story of Raj Mathur (Shahrukh Khan) and Priya Chopra (Rani Mukherjee) unfolds. The middle-class city dweller Raj meets and pursues the upper-class Priya across the countryside, Mumbai, Greece, and back in Mumbai again. The film is a modern-day tale about two people who meet and fall in love and attempt to make their relationship work amidst family politics and the highs and lows of domestic finances.

When Raj loses Priya's telephone number after their first meeting he goes looking for her across the city through the song 'Ghum shudda' (Lost person), playbacked by Sonu Nigam. Raj, together with his neighbours and friends, drawn from the spectrum of his under-, working-, lower-middle, middle-class and mixed-caste neighbourhood, literally sings and dances his away through the city as he asks the people of Mumbai to help him find Priya. With him are a homeless drunk, a traffic policeman, a postman, a shopkeeper, and the *dhobi* (clothes washman), who take to the streets, involving members of the public in their search for Priya. Claiming the urban space through songs, music, dance and *masti* (mischief and fun) is part of the message of this song, as is the disruptive potential of the common public when it takes to the streets in matters close to its heart—the song ends with the road traffic coming to a halt, much to the anguish of beeping vehicle drivers, of whom one also happens to be Priya. The couple are united again.

SINGING FOR INDIA

Songs, music and dance are integral to the narrative and its progression in Bollywood movies, and are essential aesthetic features of the films. They draw on a stock of Indian cultural and social references which are elaborated through aural and visual spectacles. The impact of *HAHK* is in its song and dance numbers, and their skilful crafting by the film's production team.[20] Predominantly, contemporary Bollywood adheres to fantasies and representations of middle-class Indian lifestyles through which tensions of tradition and modernity are played out. Although it is acknowledged that this is the dominant India that Bollywood is 'singing for' it is not the only India and it is not unproblematically represented or received. Bollywood represents an ideal India in the collective imagination, not the real, problematised nation but the shared cultural fantasy of an idealised India that is constantly striven for. The disjunction between the aspirational India of Bollywood and the actual and complex lived realities of its diverse audiences remains to be fully explored. Even within the films themselves, the contradiction between the 'fantasy'

India and the 'real' India is constantly left suspended and unresolved. It is often this very interplay that drives song and dance in Bollywood cinema and makes it a lynchpin of film culture.

In fact, the film song is not only central to film culture and to music culture, but it has become a significant aspect of diasporic Indian and diasporic South Asian life. Across India, beggars perform film hits in the streets and on the trains, and film songs blare out over loudspeakers to mark national holidays and religious festivals. At Indian wedding parties throughout the world children imitate the dance steps of the stars as a band plays cover versions of film hits. In England, on Birmingham's Soho Road and in West London's Southall Broadway, Bollywood songs play while British Asians shop and eat. And, on British Asian radio stations, film music plays endlessly across the airwaves of the diaspora. The multifarious reality of India and its diasporic culture is a far cry from the idealised middle-class paradigm seen in contemporary Bollywood, yet this shared fantasy provides a link between these diverse communities in ways yet to be fully analysed. Not only do the playback singers and the stars of Bollywood 'sing for India', but the Bollywood audience, in India and throughout the world, joins in the song.

READING POPULAR HINDI FILMS IN THE DIASPORA AND THE PERFORMANCE OF URBAN INDIAN AND DIASPORIC IDENTITY

This chapter considers some aspects of the role and representation of the diaspora in Bollywood cinema. It offers a reading of the film *Pardes* (Foreign Land, dir. Subhash Ghai, 1997) as following in a line of movies that marked the arrival of the diasporic in contemporary Bollywood cinema. It uses qualitative responses from semi-structured interviews that were conducted in an attempt to understand young British Asian viewers' engagement with recent Hindi films that encompass representations about diasporic South Asians.[1] Rather than make readings *of Pardes* through film theory and the context of its production and reception alone, I have also taken into account my respondents' readings of the audio-visual signs that they comprehended while viewing the film. In this way I attempt to open up a dialogic assessment of *Pardes* by amalgamating text-based readings with the audience response.

This chapter then moves on to consider the emergence of a particular kind of Bollywood star who has risen to prominence in tandem with the growth in production of contemporary urban Indian and diaspora-themed films. The case study of the urban/diasporic Indian character—most popularly played by current leading man Shahrukh Khan—is taken up as revealing an insight into the workings of the star system in Bollywood cinema, both in the context of globalisation and in the context of the kinds of performances that he makes possible through his enactment of urban and diasporic Indian representations in the Bollywood cinematic assemblage.

LOCATING *PARDES*: FILM BACKGROUND

Pardes follows in a line of big screen spectaculars from the nineties that were made keeping in mind both the Indian middle class and the diasporic Indian audiences. Such movies are appealing not only in terms of the big budgets spent on them affording them the most renowned directors, producers, music directors, scriptwriters, play-back singers, actors and actresses, and production teams all working together to produce memorable cinema, but also because of the lure of the thematic content of the motion pictures which cross subcontinental and diasporic boundaries.

Film-makers in Mumbai took note of the themes that were clicking with audiences at home and overseas and the potential to develop storylines that could reach across continents. In this way the diaspora, and in particular Britain, became classified as one of Bollywood's key distribution territories. The distribution of Bollywood films is divided along six territories: five in India and the sixth as the 'overseas territory' (see Ganti 2004: 56–62).[2] A film is classified as a block-buster if it makes twice the amount invested in each territory. Britain is now classified as a territory and the Bollywood film industry is keener than ever for maximum exposure of a new film overseas, anticipating that it will attract large audiences and revenue, contributing to its status as a blockbuster. With globalisation and the diaspora very much part of Indian society—from holiday travels to visit kith and kin, business trips for the middle and professional classes, exchange of cultural commodities, and the increasing gap between rich and poor—film-makers were apt in capturing these uneven flows and routes on to the big screen.

A quick glance at a few of the movies that have proved popular with Bollywood-goers in Britain in recent years include: *Dilwale Dulhaniya Le Jayenge* or *DDLJ* (The Braveheart Will Take the Bride, dir. Yash Chopra, 1995) in which a rich and spoilt British Asian boy (Shahrukh Khan) falls for a British Asian girl (Kajol) on an inter-rail trek across Europe, and then follows her to India to win over her family in accepting their marriage;[3] *Pardes* as discussed in this chapter; *Aa Ab Laut Chalen* (Come Let Us Return, dir. Rishi Kapoor, 1998), set in the US is about the dreams of a young lower middle-class graduate Rohan (Akshaye Khanna) who finds it hard to get a job in India and thus migrates to New York in search of a better life.

There he finds crass materialism amongst the South Asian bourgeoisie, and love and simpleton ways, albeit in clichés, amongst the migrant working classes in New York's Jackson Heights. To complicate matters he discovers that his father (played by seventies Bollywood star Rajesh Khanna), who was thought to be dead, is now a wealthy American businessman who also left India in search of a better life. During his travels Rohan meets and falls in love with Pooja (Aishwarya Rai). The film ends by contemplating what is lost and found on the road to making one's riches and leaving the motherland behind. Some other films which invariably deal with middle-class India and the diaspora include: *Kuch Kuch Hota Hai* (Something is Happening, dir. Karan Johar, 1998), *Hum Dil De Chuke Sanam* (I Have Given My Heart Away My Love, dir. Sanjay Leela Bhansali, 1999), *Phir Bhi Dil Hai Hindustani* (Still the Heart is Indian, dir. Aziz Mizra, 2000), *Dil Chahta Hai* (What the Heart Desires, dir. Farhan Akhtar, 2001). In the new millennium the list continues to develop.

Since the nineties Bollywood films with diasporic interests have developed the theme of migrancy and settlement in Hindi cinema from earlier years. Most notably, films of the sixties and seventies dealt with the representation of migrants from India to overseas. Films of this period invariably cast those who went abroad in side roles or as villains, depicting them as harbingers of the bad ways of the West—a corrupting influence, or counter-reference to Indian values. As director Govind Nihalani reflecting on the change of diasporic characters in a magazine interview put it:

> The camera would start from those new shoes and tilt up, the trousers, the face with the cigarette hanging from the mouth. The foreign-returned had an affected manner, the girl had bobbed hair, a mini skirt. They had lost their Indianness and become alien (Jain and Chowdhury 1997).

This image was perhaps best captured in, and often quoted in other movies after Manoj Kumar's version of *Purab Aur Paschim* (East and West, 1970), in which Saira Banu plays the wild Western girl with blonde wig who is tamed by the hero at the interval and becomes a Hindustani girl.

The eighties continued this trend of 'the West as bad' amidst angry heroes who were fighting against corruption and coming to terms with social upheavals within India and its role in the capitalist world order. In contrast, Bollywood of the nineties took note of the non-resident Indians (NRIs) as cosmopolitan in mind, speaking in English or American accents, but with their hearts and souls in the right place, i.e., respecting all things Indian. Film plots since the nineties have spanned several cities across several continents with diasporic characters taking centre stage. Film sets and costumes began to illustrate a look and feel of urban centres (openly displaying the brand names of Coca-Cola, Ralph Lauren, Nike, etc.) in which the characters could be in middle-class India or the urban diaspora of the West thereby opening up affinities with audiences across the globe. However, film critics in India have questioned some of the more city-centric film gloss which has been on the ascendancy in some of the big movies since the nineties as ignoring the plight of rural India and its culture (Chopra 1997a).

Pardes was released worldwide in August 1997 in the run-up to the celebrations marking India's 50 years of Independence on 15 August. It started off to a slow but steady reception in India and then had a successful run for several months on end, particularly in the urban centres ('Film Reviews', *India Today*, 10 November 1997). In Britain it was an instant hit and remained on the big screen for months. For instance, the film was still showing at the Piccadilly cinema in Birmingham, UK, in March 1998. In the US too it was reported as doing well with Bollywood audiences on the East and West Coast.[4]

Pardes' favoured reception amongst three main distribution territories can be accredited to its thematic content: a modern-day love story across the nation state and cultural boundaries of India and the US. The film's main publicity image on hoardings, posters and music album sleeves distributed around the world is interesting. The film poster reads 'American Dreams, Indian Soul' (see Figure 3.1). Its hero and heroine embrace each other in the middle of a still which captures a pre-9/11 New York skyline on one side and the Taj Mahal on the other, set beneath atmospheric clouds of change. The 'American dreams' are those of the heroine Ganga (Mahima Chaudhary) who contemplates new horizons, and the 'Indian soul' is that of the hero Arjun (Shahrukh Khan) who, although an American citizen, is still attached to the motherland (India). As the title and publicity of the film suggest, *Pardes* captures well many of the sensibilities which constitute the diasporic subject: displacement, new

Figure 3.1: Film poster of *Pardes* with the hero Arjun (Shahrukh Khan) and heroine Ganga (Mahima Chaudhary)

beginnings and issues of belonging and alienation. Such sensibilities proved popular amongst the film's urban Indian and diasporic audiences, who themselves were experiencing social and cultural shifts in their attendant societies which were undergoing modernisation.

Another possible reason for the film's popularity was the fact that it was Subhash Ghai's brain child. Ghai wrote the story and screenplay, and independently produced and directed it under his banner of Mukta Arts Films, a private limited production and distribution company based in Mumbai. Ghai has often been dubbed 'one of the few great showmen' of contemporary Bollywood cinema in the South Asian entertainment press working on only one film at a time and producing memorable big-screen spectaculars (see Rajadhyaksha and Willemen 1994: 95 for brief career history and filmography of Ghai). *Pardes* was released four years after Ghai's last film *Khalnayak* (The Villain, 1993) which had attracted censorship problems in India because of the performance of the erotically charged song 'Choli ke peeche kya hai?' (What is beneath the blouse?). This song was written by lyricist Anand Bakshi to the music of Laxmikant and Pyarelal and provocatively enacted on screen by the then leading Bollywood actress Madhuri Dixit. Interestingly, the track 'Choli ke peeche kya hai?' was an instant hit across India and in Britain too where it was successfully re-mixed by Bally Sagoo on his 1994 *Bollywood Flashback* album with Columbia records. Thus, being produced and directed under the auspices of Subhash Ghai, *Pardes* was an anticipated film.

Briefly, the story of *Pardes* is as follows: Arjun (Shahrukh Khan) is the adopted son of American NRI billionaire Kishori Lal (Amrish Puri) who is sent to India to help arrange the marriage between Ganga (Mahima Chaudhary), Kishori Lal's lifelong friend Sooraj Dev's (Alok Nath) daughter, and his adoptive father's biological son Rajiv (Apurva Agnihotri). Rajiv, however, is far from the perfect bridegroom for Ganga—he tries to rape her whilst on a pre-marital visit to Las Vegas. Through a series of star-crossed encounters spanning India and the US Arjun and Ganga fall in love. At the end of the film, and having convinced parents on both sides of the family that they are right for each other, Arjun and Ganga are married.

READING *PARDES*

Pardes was recalled by my respondents as one of the most recent films they had seen either at the cinema hall or on video, and one which they had enjoyed and were therefore able to discuss. As a result of the extended interviews the following themes emerged through which my respondents made sense of and related to the film *Pardes*: *Pardes* as a commentary on South Asia and the diaspora; the role of the female character Ganga; and the love story of Ganga and Arjun.

'Pardes' as Text on South Asia and the Diaspora

The story of *Pardes* is set across a village in Dehradun (north-east of the capital New Delhi) in India, and sporadically over North America and Canada, though most notably on the west coast of the US in Los Angeles. In essence the film is a meditation on the union and relationship between Indians in India and Indians living overseas in the urban centres of the West in the contemporary period. Although the Indian diaspora depicted in the film is one set in the US and is very class specific—Kishori Lal's family is the richest of the South Asian-Americans—my respondents identified the film as a general commentary on South Asian cultural values and traditions, and their translations in the diaspora in Britain too.

RD: What did you think of *Pardes*?

Reshmo: I really liked *Pardes* because it was basically trying to tell you about your roots and everything.

Babs: I liked that because that was more the way things really are, you know, I could relate with the film more rather than those with jumping around in a field and singing songs in it which doesn't really happen (laughs).

Madhuri: I think it was a brilliant film, it's the kind of film you can watch again and again and pick up something new each time. There was just something about it.

Nahid: I think it was talking about British Asians more, the main actress she's come from abroad, she's experiencing how we are supposed to live here, it's totally different, she finds it hard to adapt to the life here, and the film addresses the issues why in its own way.

References to the US in the film, either through direct location shots or through dialogue, acknowledge it as 'the big brother' of world socio-political relations, but the US is also used to invoke 'the West' more generally. The opening credits of the film are interesting in this respect. As my respondent Bally said: 'You knew the film was different and that it was going to deal with British and Indian experiences because right from the start when the titles come up it shows shots of India and abroad.'

The credits in *Pardes* role with images of US skyscrapers, lit up against a night sky, and are interspersed with images from India, most notably with rural village landscapes thereby setting up a contrast between East and West. Arjun is briefly shown and so too is Ganga on either side of the Atlantic, both contemplating their ideal partners. Arjun is seen painting a picture of an Indian woman in rural attire and Ganga is on the river shores lost in thought. The contrast between East and West is not as clichéd as one might easily assume but is rather intriguing, one that is carefully put together by the film's artistic team under Subhash Ghai's direction. The editing of shots between the US (*pardes* or foreign land) and India (*des* or homeland) is not abrupt or obtrusive but smooth. They follow and flow into one another and have been skilfully handled by Renu Saluja, the film's editor.

The opening credits are supported by a moving music score which changes mood according to the images on screen and has been composed by music directors Nadeem and Shravan and Vanraj Bhatia who arranged the background music. The music signals both *pardes* and *des* in different but connected ways. The US is depicted as overwhelming by the sheer size of its buildings and the people as anonymous amidst the million others who dwell there. South Asians in the US are shown as being there primarily for work and better livelihoods and this is affirmed through the images of the industrial workplace with the music pounding away to replicate the sounds of manual and automated machinery. India, on the other hand, is shown as the land left behind which is poor, simple and scenic, at least in its rural form. Even then, the film makes constant reference to the changing pace of development as it trickles into the rural setting amongst those who can afford it. A large wind powered electricity-generating fan and a satellite communication dish adorn Ganga's parental home in the village. The constant oscillation between the images of *pardes* (US) and *des* (India/homeland)—and the fact that the film's main protagonists are located in the two different worlds and yet are contemplating their ideal partners where ever they may be—link the two protagonists together in complex ways which is commensurate with the diasporic condition. For one can be located, geographically, in one part of the world but yet be culturally affiliated and rooted in a social system/tradition which may be elsewhere, miles away.

As the opening credits come to a close an Air India jumbo jet is seen landing in India with the voice-over of Kishori Lal (Amrish Puri) rusing over his affectionate bonds with his motherland:

> It's been 35 years since I have been living in America. Every time I return to India I get excited. It is like I'm returning into the lap of my mother ... I do not care whether India may or may not have much, but one thing it surely has is love.

The final image of the credits is the Taj Mahal, built by the Moghul emperor Shah Jahan in memory of his beloved wife Mumtaz Mahal, an internationally recognised monument celebrating the ideal of love. In this way the romantic story set across *pardes* and *des* is set into motion and the credits function explicitly to narrate the contents of the movie to the viewer.

The film *Pardes*, both as a commentary on the relationships between South Asians in the subcontinent and South Asians overseas, was welcomed and critically appreciated by my respondents. As the following responses illustrate:

Taran: Like Mahima's (the actress who plays Ganga) parents' house, did you see how big and fantastic that was? They obviously weren't the poor family from the normal village, but also it was nice to see them in that setting because India isn't just all about poverty.

Bally: The family in America, on the whole they came across as completely American apart from one or two of the characters. They really didn't like India at all, or things Indian. I thought that that was a bit extreme to show them like that but then you do get people who turn their back on their own culture and people.

Kully: Like when I watched *Pardes* I asked my mum is this how it is in India, how it's shown in the film. Sometimes she agrees with the film, at other times she doesn't. If she doesn't then I'll just take it in for myself and it's interesting to see how they portray India and Indian things.

The desire to see the complex and multifaceted nature of South Asians in and through representation was very strong in my respondents. The images in *Pardes*, both complex and clichéd, which represented South Asian characters were simultaneously acknowledged and contested by my respondents. The images helped them understand their own perceptions of South Asians as predominantly backward and poverty-stricken as often portrayed in the Western mainstream media. In particular, the role of the female character Ganga emerged as a talking point in the interviews through which the respondents made sense of a number of social messages that the film was relaying.

Ganga: The Woman of *Des* and *Pardes*

The role of the character Ganga in *Pardes* serves two purposes. At an obvious and basic level Ganga is the female romantic lead of the film. More importantly, her character functions as a way of understanding the move towards a union between *des* and *pardes*, particularly as experienced by a young Indian woman. Ganga is very much the central character of the film. In fact, Subhash Ghai in an Indian film magazine interview recalls how he initially thought of naming the film 'Ganga' (see 'Midas Reclaims His Touch', *Movie*, September 1997: 26–29). One respondent Taran, made an explicit link with the story of Ganga's travel from India to the US, to get married and start a new life, as one that resonated with the experiences of her mother. In Taran's words,

> *Pardes* was so true, my mum's a *pardesan* [female foreigner], she came from India, she's come to *pardes* now. To her this [the UK] is her *pardes*. People do go abroad, get married, settled down or whatever, so it does happen.

Ganga, played by Mahima Chaudhary in her debut role, is depicted in a complex way that addresses the dual sensibilities of being both Indian and Western according to the context. In India Ganga is shown to be the essence of the rural Indian woman—innocent and virginal. The name Ganga is itself an explicit reference to the river Ganges in India, thereby immediately conjuring images of the rural idyll and a strong attachment to gendered notions of landscape. Ganga is often picturised running through green fields and playing with younger children by the riverside. She is also the darling of her household playing beloved granddaughter and daughter to her grandmother and parents respectively, and elder sibling to her brothers and sisters. However, whilst Ganga emanates the rural ideal she is also a graduate in English Literature, competent in speaking English and fully capable of using modern communication and technology. Ganga's house in the village is equipped with all the facilities available in urban homes such as televisions, videos, computers, and mobile phones, but in the film these are always present in the background in a matter of fact way and are rarely seen used. Through this imagery Ganga becomes the personification of an ideal of modern India—educated and literate in the contemporary world but attune to her cultural values which are very much Indian. Ganga is able to switch easily between the two worlds of India and the US in terms of dress and language but her heart remains with India. Reshmo, a respondent, noticed the way Ganga was characterised through her costumes:

RD: What did you think about the role of the character Ganga in the film, played by Mahima?

Reshmo: She was really nice actually. The outfits she was wearing compared to other films was really nice, and she was a new actress in that film, it was her first film, so the way the outfits and that brought her out was really good.

Ganga's costumes adhere to the traditional layout of the salwar kameez yet they are modern in their aesthetic and cut. Even when Ganga is adorned in white garments signifying purity of heart and virginity, she also dons a bright scarf around her neck and dazzling jewellery which suggests there is more to her than meets the eye. In the more dramatic and confrontational scenes the colours of her dresses are bright and daring; oranges and reds are used to good effect, and in the song and dance sequences her costumes flow freely according to her movements. Ganga is not restricted in any easy sense either through characterisation by Mahima Chaudhary or by the audio-visual signs that accompany her on screen. My respondents acknowledged the character of Ganga as defying easy dichotomies of tradition and modernity and as challenging stereotypical notions of Indian femininity as passive (see Figure 3.2).

Babs: She [Ganga] knew what she wanted and what she didn't want. She wasn't portrayed as some, you know, poor defenceless girl who didn't know how to cope. She wanted to go to America, she wasn't forced, but when she was being forced to do things she stood up for herself which was good.

Reshmo: I found when she [Ganga] was in India she wasn't all that strong, maybe because she was surrounded by her own people. But when she went to America she was largely on her own and I reckon she came across a lot stronger than compared to when she was in India.

Madhuri: Some British Asians probably thought she [Ganga] was a typical village girl, which was probably true in some sense in the way she was portrayed, but I think there was more to her character than that. Like she was right in her own way when she was putting her foot down and saying she wouldn't do certain things that she didn't like.

Figure 3.2: Ganga (Mahima Chaudhary) as the village girl in India and in cosmopolitan dress in the US

Ganga leaves her parental home for the US with the intention of marrying Rajiv and starting a new life. However, upon his return to America, Rajiv continues to see his girlfriends, appears to be an alcoholic, and even forces himself upon Ganga for pre-marital sex. It becomes clear that Rajiv is the extreme opposite of Ganga and the worst example of Western hedonism. As Rajiv sums up for Ganga the idea of individualism in America: 'In America if people want to be left alone, we leave them alone.' When Rajiv and Ganga occupy the same frame on screen they are depicted as polar opposites in their body language and attitude towards each other. As one of my respondents said:

> Kully: The American guy was totally the bad American guy, brought up looking down on people, thinking Indians were rubbish. The Indian girl was brought up the traditional way and that's why she was different to the American guy.

In the attempted rape scene between Rajiv and Ganga, Ganga refuses to become an easy victim. She is signalled as a fighting goddess who knocks out the drunken assailant and manages to hold back her anger in time and avoid stabbing him with a knife.

The Arjun and Ganga Love Story: When *Pardes* is Possible

Meanwhile, Arjun and Ganga are brought closer together in a world in which making money is given priority and people's feelings and relationships are marginalised. Their coming together is gradual and not enforced. They both discover what it is to love one another— largely mutual respect—and the film consists of many scenes in which their love is tested right until the film's end. One scene that was recalled by more than one respondent was Arjun's birthday party.

> Reshmo: I remember the scene when she left her fiancé's family in America and went to Shahrukh Khan's birthday party, to wish him a happy birthday, which went against the family's wishes.

And as Nahid and Madhuri said:

> Nahid: Like going to Shahrukh Khan's birthday party isn't something expected from a girl who has just come from India, you know, and going to a male friend's party.

> Madhuri: Though that would depend from where you came from, the village or the city. I think the film was trying to say we don't all come from mud huts you know.

Arjun decides to spend his birthday alone away from his close friends and, in particular, away from Ganga whom he dare not admit he loves. Ganga and Arjun's best friends plan a birthday party for him, much to his surprise. Halfway during the party Rajiv's aunt phones Ganga and argues with her urging her to come home immediately. Ganga flatly refuses and Arjun and Ganga's declaration of love for each other is announced through the song and dance of 'Meri mehbooba' (My beloved, playbacked by Kumar Sanu and Alka Yagnik).

Like most Bollywood films of the romantic genre the love match between the hero and heroine has to 'work' if it is to be believed and appreciated by audiences. The genre of romantic films sets up an expectation amongst its audiences: they know that a couple will be matched, obstacles placed in their way, but their union will almost always be achieved by the film's end. However, innovative film-makers are ever more eager to excite their audiences either by casting different actors to play the same storyline in different ways, or by adding new, additional elements and twists to the traditional love story. In *Pardes* the love story of Arjun and Ganga is complicated by two factors: Ganga is already in the process of an arranged marriage to Rajiv before they meet; and, Ganga and Arjun's coming together must bridge the cultural distance between *des* and *pardes*. For my respondents, at least, the Arjun–Ganga love story worked not only because the love of the two characters was depicted as undying and true in a chivalric sense, but also because the story offered a balanced depiction of the two families involved.

RD: What was it about *Pardes* that was so special for you?
Nahid: When Shahrukh Khan fell in love with the girl [She laughs]. The way Shahrukh Khan helps her out through every difficulty is really brilliant. I really liked the scene in *Pardes* when Mahima turns round to him and says 'Look at yourself. I want someone like you!' and the way he was stunned by that phrase I think he looked really nice there. And the way she says it is really good as well, I think she acted really well.

Bally: The love story was different because they [Arjun and Ganga] weren't necessarily going against the family's wishes. Even when they knew they liked each other they kept apart but they only really came together when they had their parent's approval on either side. They had to win them over, and the American guy just wasn't right for her.

After Rajiv's rape attempt, Ganga escapes and seeks Arjun's help and together they leave America and return to India as persons in exile to Ganga's parents home. Rajiv in the meantime lies to his family about why Ganga has left, accusing Arjun of eloping with her. Kishori Lal telephones Suraj Dev and blames Arjun. Sooraj Dev in turn becomes enraged and refuses to hear Arjun and Ganga's story. He attacks Arjun and banishes him from his house. Arjun leaves with Ganga in pursuit challenging him to stay on and marry her. Rajiv returns to India to take Ganga back and hires hoodlums to attack Arjun. Kishori Lal also arrives in India and, together with Suraj Dev's family, they also go after Arjun, Ganga and Rajiv to confront them. The closing scenes of the film are interesting not least because of their exciting build up to a climax which keeps the spectator engaged and guessing as to how the film will conclude, but also as they bring together the whole family across three generations to resolve what went wrong in the union of *pardes* and *des*, and to decide who Ganga will end up marrying.

Ganga's grandmother or *Daadi* (played by Dina Pathak), Ganga's parents, Kishori Lal, Arjun, Rajiv and Ganga are all present in the deciding moment of the film. Ganga explains the trials she has been put through as a daughter, daughter-in-law to be, and prospective wife. She even uncovers her shoulder to reveal the bruises inflicted on her by Rajiv when he tries to rape her. However, Ganga refuses to unilaterally decide whether to leave Rajiv and be with Arjun. She does not wish to be the lone radical in bringing about change and in reconciling the union between *des* and *pardes*. She interpolates all those present as responsible for the predicament she is in and asks for a concerted effort by them to correct the wrongs and do the right thing. Else she is ready to sacrifice her hopes and desires by marrying Rajiv who will do no more than consume her and cast her aside. As the following translated dialogue from the final scenes of the film illustrates:

> Ganga: [To the parents] If you tell me to jump into this fire then I will, because you are our parents. If you tell me to drink this poison then I will.
>
> Daadi: [Cutting in] Why should you drink this poison, why should you?! For years women have been drinking poison. First listen to your parents, then listen to your husband, then your children. You will definitely not drink this poison.

Suraj Dev: Mother you keep out of this.

Daadi: You keep quiet! You have made a mockery out of your daughter, the lot of you. [To Kishori Lal] Kishori Lal you used to go around singing 'my land is India, my duty is India'. You wanted to send a daughter of India to America, you wanted to settle India in America. Well you really have done well haven't you?! I ask you Kishori Lal why try and set up something which does not match, which has no matching rhythm or beat?

Daadi represents the oldest of the three generations and in the earlier scenes of the film is seen as quietly reading the Bhagavad Gita (holy book of the Hindus). By implication one might be tempted to interpret her character as firmly rooted in 'tradition' and as a preserver of culture in a conservative manner. However, it is Daadi who urges Ganga to pursue Arjun once he has been thrown out of the house by Suraj Dev, and it is Daadi who staunchly criticises the manipulation of women whilst fulfilling their roles in a patriarchal society. Surprisingly, Daadi goes one step further than Ganga and uses her position as the family elder to speak above everybody else, including the men. Instead of endorsing cultural tradition she sets about to alter it. According to her Rajiv and Ganga's union is impossible as there is no respect or love in their relationship, they are at odds with one another and have 'no matching rhythm or beat'. They represent the irreconcilable ends of *pardes* and *des* respectively. In contrast, Arjun and Ganga not only love each other and are comfortable in the ways of *pardes* (the US), minus its excesses, they also respect and communicate the ideals of *des* (India) and are therefore poised for a union that is bound to last. Daadi's timely intervention prompts Kishori Lal to slap Rajiv and condemn him back to America and together with Suraj Dev agree that Arjun and Ganga be married and begin their new lives in America together.

The film *Pardes* ends with the union of Arjun and Ganga on Indian soil but with the end credits displaying images of their new life together as a married couple in America. In this way the diaspora in *pardes* is possible without having to compromise how one is constituted as a South Asian in terms of relationships and customs with the *des* and by neither having to give up a new found identity, nor the creation of new cultures in the West. Furthermore *Pardes* advocates for a new place of settlement in which love and respect for one another is given paramount importance and crass individualism is avoided by learning through dialogue with elders as well as peers. *Pardes*, then, is as much a movie about the notion of home for South Asians living in the diasporas of the West as it is about the renewal and remaking of the West through affiliations with and visits to South Asia in collaboration with one another. My respondents took pleasure not only from the 'happy ending' of the film but also the way in which it related to some of their own familial connections across *des* and *pardes*:

> Bally: I enjoyed the ending because it didn't isolate the family members from each other. It was basically saying people have to come together and work their differences through rather than diss the family set up which I really liked. Being able to keep in touch with your family in India is important and I could relate to that.

> Rita: Shahrukh and Mahima were allowed to get married and go back to America as well as have that connection with the family in India, rather than be cut off. That was nice.

> Manjit: The ending was a bit utopian perhaps, you know, another happy ending in Bollywood [smiles]. But it made me think about India, Britain, America or wherever and how I could be connected with these places.

> RD: How do you mean? Could you say a bit more?

> Manjit: You know, like my relations who are settled there and how we might relate with each other, our differences and outlooks, stuff like that.

Although my respondents and my own analysis of *Pardes* have paid attention to the fluid diasporic representations and possibilities inherent in the film there are other readings possible; for example, of the role of the Daadi character and the way in which the climax of the film ultimately works. For instance, one could argue that the film uses a hegemonic resolve in which 'all is well', the patriarchal family structure is adhered to, and conservative male and female gendered roles are kept intact. In this way one could argue that the film's moral and social ideological agendas are left unchallenged. For example, Patricia Uberoi (1998) in her readings of *Dilwale Dulhaniya Le Jayenge* (*DDLJ*) and *Pardes* considers the male NRI/diasporic figure, at best, as a response to threats to Indian identity in the age of globalisation wherein the nation is re-imagined through the sympathetic attachments that he has to the homeland. Purnima

Mankekar in her reading of *DDLJ* argues that the film privileges the Indian male's agency by casting him in the figure of the economically mobile NRI and guardian of the Indian woman's sexual purity, thus replaying the classic woman/nation conflation (Mankekar 1999: 750–51).[5] Both authors further consider the depiction of women's protest in diasporic-themed films such as *DDLJ* and *Pardes* that challenge the injustice of tradition. However, they both discount any subversive potential that is rendered by such a challenge and point to the patriarchal negotiation that takes place between the father and prospective male suitor before marriage approval is given to the two lovers. This, for them, casts the woman as an object to be socially transacted. On the other hand, Jyotika Virdi inserts the issue of feminist agency that is overlooked by these two authors and argues that this is important in terms of understanding how the films give agency to the young couple in terms of pickin a romantic partner which contravenes social conventions (Virdi 2003: 198). Contributing to these interpretations of films such as *Pardes*, my own argument—drawing on an understanding of the way in which my respondents made sense of the film—argues that one-off readings of such Bollywood films, as in the case of Uberoi and Mankekar, need to be left open-ended. As indicated by my respondents the film *Pardes* is a polysemic text, laden with multiple meanings about South Asia and its diaspora (for example, how does one belong?), and about the characters who signify particular ideals and non-ideals (for instance, Arjun and Rajiv). As with any other cinematic text, Bollywood films are also invested with meanings, ideological or otherwise, and like any other cinematic audience Bollywood audiences read the films in different ways. My respondents made sense of *Pardes* as a film containing elements of reality and fantasy and their articulations as coming together to offer the audience a flexible understanding and construction of diasporic sensibilities and familial connections in Britain, South Asia and elsewhere.

This chapter, then, has so far considered the depiction of the diaspora in Bollywood films, focusing on the case study of the film *Pardes*. Whilst Bollywood has and increasingly does take on board representations relating to the South Asian diaspora these are themselves refracted in Bollywood cinema through an idiosyncratic understanding of the relationship between the homeland and its diaspora. In this relationship clichés such as the myth of return to the motherland are often played out, as also the ideas and representations that profess more fluid social possibilities about the diasporic condition. As the extracts from my respondents indicate, the clichés are not taken on board unproblematically. They are reinterpreted and translated in the light of the actual diasporic contexts in which Bollywood audiences find themselves, whether in the UK or elsewhere and read these films as offering select possibilities in the formation of their subjectivities.

THE URBAN/DIASPORIC BOLLYWOOD STAR

This chapter now considers another important factor contributing to the rise of the appeal of Bollywood cinema throughout urban centres in India and in the diaspora: that of the role of a particular kind of film star who is able to communicate with both constituencies simultaneously. The star system in Bollywood cinema is perhaps the most important starting point in terms of film inception right from production through to its perceived success at the box office. In fact, the star system in Bollywood is a more crucial feature of the production process than in Hollywood cinema; more often than not, the star and increasingly the male hero is a more important consideration for producers and directors than the other stages of the production process.

Commenting on the star system in popular Hindi cinema and in an analysis of perhaps the most well known of Bollywood stars of all time, Amitabh Bachchan, Mishra (2002) draws on the work of Dyer (1979) and Ellis (1982) about the construction of the Hollywood star as a heuristic model that is summarised in the following ways:

1. the star's roles should be examined in regard to a culture's precursor text(s);
2. through these manifold roles or narrative placements on screen a star gradually accumulates his or her own symbolic biography;
3. the screen biography and the star's actual life intersect, often generating industry deals and occasional political placements;
4. the star is a material phenomenon, a physical body with idiosyncratic or stereotypical voice, physiognomy, gestural repertoire, physical agility, and costume; and,

5. the star is iconic whose public reception is manifested in shrines, calendar art, comics, T-shirts, and so on.

Mishra goes on to advance this model in order to account for the Indian star, considering further an analysis of the song and dialogic situations that constitute two overarching systems that lead to the construction of the star in popular Hindi cinema (Mishra 2002: 126–27). For Mishra, Bachchan can be considered as 'the actor as parallel text' (ibid.: Chapter 5) whose star persona exists in and beyond the diegesis and also in the real life drama of the actor as a parallel and often simultaneous activity. Mishra analyses the formation of Bachchan's stardom through his on-screen persona as the angry young man of Indian cinema that is a halfway house between the heroic and anti-heroic virtues as found in the Hindu epic of the Mahabharata. He outlines the star's alleged romantic affair with the actress Rekha that was widely reported in fanzines and the tabloids. He reports on how large parts of India came to a standstill when the actor was rushed into hospital and operated on after being seriously hurt during the shooting of a fight sequence on the sets of a film. Bachchan's formal entry into Indian politics as a parliamentary candidate during 1985–87, surrounded in controversy of bribery and corruption but never proven, is also discussed. And, the use of song and dialogue by Bachchan is finally put forward as testimony to how these two features act as the key modes of identification through which narrative and identificatory transactions occur between the Indian star and spectator. Bachchan is well known for his appropriation of Indian folk songs, for his articulate command of the Hindi language and for his imposing voice that has delivered some of the most memorable dialogues in Hindi cinema, especially in action and melodramatic sequences. In this way, for Mishra, Bachchan transcends the status of stardom and becomes a text in his own right.

Rather than follow Mishra's heuristic model and offer a reading of Shahrukh Khan as another parallel text, I would rather examine the construction and performance of Shahrukh Khan in two related ways. First, to consider Shahrukh Khan as a type of an Indian star who, since the mid-nineties, has been able to command an interesting relationship with both urban India and the diaspora. Second, to offer a reading of Shahrukh Khan as a literal and metaphorical embodiment of an actor-cum-star who is able to perform most successfully the anxieties, hopes and fantasies of urban India and its related South Asian diasporas. This approach differs from Mishra's as it offers a close reading of the star not only by focusing on the on- and off-screen capabilities of the actor alone, but by also drawing attention to the ways in which the star is constructed and achieves a material phenomenon with and through the assistance of film technology and its wider articulations in the cinematic assemblage.

Shahrukh Khan: An Urban/Diasporic Indian Phenomenon

Shahrukh Khan has emerged in the millennium as the premier actor of the moment in popular Hindi cinema. He is sought after by film producers and directors alike for their big budget films, he has a host of adulating fans around the world and is one of the few actors to command the highest acting fees in Bollywood. He has also signed endorsements with Pepsi and Airtel Communications thereby securing lucrative financial deals with them through advertising and brand association. He has also, together with actress Juhi Chawla and Bollywood film director Aziz Mizra, ventured into film production with the launch of their media production company Dreamz Unlimited.

Shahrukh Khan started his media career in television. It was his role in the television series *Fauji* (Soldier, 1988) as the young soldier Abhimanyu that won him instant recognition. Shahrukh Khan's early film career can be characterised as strongly 'filmi'—his first films saw him give performances that were edgy, unrefined and highly melodramatic in his part as the obligatory romantic hero in a main or supporting role. In fact these were traits that he fostered well in his anti-heroic and dark roles in *Baazigar* (Player, dirs. Abbas Alibhai Burmawalla and Mastan Alibhai Burmawalla, 1993), *Anjaam* (Result, dir. Rahul Raiwal, 1994), and *Darr* (Fear, dir. Yash Chopra, 1994) through which he really rose to fame as portraying a psychotic lover. In *Darr* he stalks the character Kiran (Juhi Chawla) to the point of terror in an attempt to gain her love, and his dialogue is also constructed as part of his troubled state of mind—he is incapable of pronouncing Kiran's name without stuttering 'K-K-K-Kiran'.

A year later, in 1995, amidst his popularity as a anti-hero, Shahrukh returned to playing the romantic lead in *Dilwale Dulhania Le Jayenge* (*DDLJ*) which went on to establish him as contemporary urban India's and the diaspora's favourite hero. In fact, *DDLJ* made under the prestigious Yash Raj Films banner has become a landmark film in popular Hindi cinema marking the arrival of a trend for characters and diegetic activity that deal with issues of the homeland and the diaspora through the lens of Bollywood (Chopra 2003).

As we have seen in the discussion of the film *Pardes* earlier, Shahrukh Khan has gone on to be increasingly cast as the preferred mediator between the homeland and its diaspora. In several of his films since *DDLJ* he is seen playing the urban Indian and/or diasporic hero: *English Babu, Desi Mem* (dir. Praveen Nischol, 1996), *Yes Boss* (dir. Aziz Mirza, 1997), *Dil to Pagal Hai* (dir. Yash Chopra, 1997), *Pardes* (1997), *Kuch Kuch Hota Hai* (dir. Karan Johar, 1998), *Dil Se...* (dir. Mani Ratnam, 1998), *Phir Bhi Dil Hai Hindustani* (dir. Aziz Mirza, 2000), *Mohabbatein* (dir. Aditya Chopra, 2000), *Kabhi Kushi Khabie Gham* (dir. Karan Johar, 2001), *Devdas* (dir. Sanjay Leela Bhansali, 2002), *Chalte Chalte* (dir. Aziz Mirza, 2003), *Kal Ho Naa Ho* (dir. Nikhil Advani, 2003), *Main Hoon Na* (dir. Farah Khan, 2004) and *Swades* (dir. Ashutosh Gowariker, 2004). Other contemporary actors have also played similar roles but it is Shahrukh Khan who has captivated audiences in urban India and around the world as the favoured metropolitan Indian and NRI protagonist time and time again.

Shahrukh Khan's rise as the urban/diasporic Indian on screen has been in tandem with the circulation of Bollywood in the moment of globalisation, as is discussed throughout this book. Anne Ciecko (2001) in her study of the global appeal and marketing of the star in Bollywood cinema argues that contemporary Bollywood stars, and male stars in particular, are interfacing with the increasing capital possibilities afforded to them through advertising and tie-ins with global multinationals, and through their appearances at global film shows, and their circulation as cultural icons on the Internet. In this way the actors expand their star value and operate discursively as a 'author function' that becomes central to the nexus of production, exhibition, distribution and reception of popular Hindi films. Bollywood movies and their stars are further implicated in the diasporic formation of imagined communities, made possible through the processes of globalisation and post-colonialism (ibid.: 130–31). Ciecko goes on to outline the importance of Shahrukh Khan as a key player amidst such global, cultural and economic articulations through the example of his personal entrepreneurial website, www.SRKworld.com. Here,

Shahrukh Khan often engages, through chat, with his fans about his movies, his star image, female co-stars, rising star hero rivals, family values, and his commercial endorsements such as Pepsi. Here fans can also enquire about where and when his next national and/or international personal appearance will be, either at film promotional tours, star shows or charity functions. In this way, Shahrukh Khan, by being cyber present and vocal, is an example of Bollywood and especially of its commodified male star as being glocal—being local and global simultaneously (Ciecko 2001: 133).

Shahrukh Khan and the Performance of Urban and Diasporic Representation in Bollywood

But what of the performativity on screen that has made Shahrukh Khan the popular emissary of the global moment in Bollywood cinema that appeals to both urban India and the diaspora, thus making him transnational? To this end, we need to turn towards an analysis and reading of the ways in which Shahrukh Khan, through the cinematic assemblage of Bollywood, makes possible the desires, fantasies and anxieties of urban/diasporic India as an identity through his performances. Here, I note two lines of interdisciplinary thought that are useful as a framework for developing this kind of analysis: (i) identity as performance; and (ii) identity as represented through the medium of film.

In sociology the idea of identities as constructed through a performance of selfhood can be traced back to the work of Erving Goffman (1959) where he posits that there is a sense of theatricality to everyday life. This entails the idea that selfhood is performed through various roles and functions in particular spaces and it is through this kind of social activity that people come to assume personas, roles and take part in social performances. Goffman draws on dramaturgical references to outline the nature of social performativity but only in a metaphorical way, i.e., he uses the dramatic metaphor as a useful way of describing the way things are. In order to elaborate on the nature of social performance beyond metaphor, the work on identity as performance in Drama and Theatre Studies is perhaps a useful contribution to understanding the construction of selfhood as a constant performance. This line of thinking also allows us to think beyond selfhood as existing outside of, or in relation to, an already constituted 'real self' (see, for example, Schechner 1985).[6] Here identity and performance are understood as articulated through a reciprocating relationship wherein identities are made sense of through a performance (whether on stage and/or in actual life), which encompass an affective and tangible understanding of the identities that are being performed. Furthermore, it is often through the use and performance of the body in its actual and symbolic forms that constructions of cultural identities are rendered socially visible.

If we extend this understanding of identity as arising out of a constant performance to cinema—a performance as taking place in actual life and as also reciprocated through various media—we need to take on board how a performance of selfhood is further represented on screen through the cinematic apparatus. This incorporates acknowledging that the medium of film is about the juxtaposition of sounds and images through which the body appears and reappears in a directed manner and through which an illusion of the everyday and everyday identities are enacted with the assistance of technology (Chow 1998). This kind of enactment asserts an identifiable realism that arises from the performance of selves in the diegesis and an understanding of the performance of selves on the part of the audience as in tandem with, or incongruent to, each other. The performance of cultural or social identity through the medium of film, then, can be usefully thought of as the representation of the agile movements of the human body as captured by the technical equipment with an intended meaning, and translated in numerous possible ways by different viewers.

In order to consider Shahrukh Khan's performativity as the urban/diasporic Indian within this framework, I offer a reading of one of his hit films from the summer of 2004, *Main Hoon Na* (I'm Here Now, dir. Farah Khan). *Main Hoon Na* is the story of Major Ram Prasad Sharma (Shahrukh Khan) of the Indian Army who becomes embroiled in a series of events to ensure that 'Project *Milaap* (Unity)'—the releasing of innocent captives on either sides of the border of India and Pakistan—can take place as a sign of trust and movement towards peace between the two nations. Opposed to this project is an ex-Indian Army officer, who parades under the pseudonym of Raghavan (played by Sunil Shetty), who together with his group of ex-army militants terrorises those involved in Project *Milaap* in an attempt to prevent its occurrence. At the outset of the film Raghavan kills Ram's father, Brigadier Shekhar Sharma (played by Naseeruddin Shah), in a shoot out. On his death bed, Ram's father tells him the story of how Ram's stepmother left home with his younger stepbrother as she refused to accept Ram as the elder son in the house. It is revealed that Ram is Shekhar's illegitimate child from his affair with another woman. Shekhar pleads with Ram to find his mother and brother and to unite the separated family. Under the request of General Bakshi (played by Kabir Bedi), Ram is sent to a college in Darjeeling under the guise of a mature student to protect the General's daughter Sanjana (Amrita Rao), who has been threatened by Raghavan. As it turns out his stepmother and stepbrother are also located in the same town. Whilst at college Ram also searches for his separated stepbrother Lakshman/Lucky (played by Zayed Khan) and stepmother Madhu (played by Kiran Kher) and manages to move in with them as a paying guest with a view to fulfil his father's last wish. During the course of the film, Sanjana and Lucky fall in love and Ram falls for his chemistry teacher, Miss Chandni (played by Sushmita Sen).

The file *Main Hoon Na* has been made in the mould of a classic masala film with ample ingredients of action, romance, melodrama, and elaborate song and dance sequences. Like almost any other Bollywood masala film it too draws on one of the predominant mythic and religious texts of India, the Ramayana. Evidently, Shahrukh Khan is cast as Ram, his younger brother literally as Lakshman, the villain is a reworking of the name of the demon king Ravan, and Shahrukh Khan's role can be read as averting a threat to the nation, India. In addition, Ram also has to bring together his separated and bickering family. However, the film's creative team, headed by renowned dance choreographer Farah Khan in her directorial debut, has deliberately gone against the grain of applying this Hindu text in a right-wing nationalist vein. *Main Hoon Na* can be situated in recent popular Hindi cinema as following on from the anti-Pakistan, anti-Muslim slanted films of late such as *Gadar* (Revolution, dir. Anil Sharma, 2001) and *The Hero* (dir. Anil Sharma, 2003), both starring Sunny Deol. *Main Hoon Na* is a deliberate and conscious attempt to move away from the depiction of Pakistan as the constant wrongdoer or sole villain. Instead it reinterprets the Ramayana predominantly as a story of reconciliation and diplomacy in which India as a nation has to deal with its internal enemies and terrorists—as depicted by the character Raghavan—who pose a threat to the possible peace process between India and Pakistan. The allegory of Ram's bickering family unit, a metaphor for the social condition of the nation, must also be restored through dialogue and love.

Shahrukh Khan's role in *Main Hoon Na* follows his trajectory as a mediating signifier, especially one that shifts between the homeland and the diaspora. In his previous films that have been popular with diaspora audiences we see him cast invariably as mediating relationships and social disputes of sorts across nation state boundaries, whether in *DDLJ*, *Pardes*, *Mohabbatein* or *Kal Ho Naa Ho*. In *Main Hoon Na* he has the additional complex task of ensuring that Project *Milaap* will take off with a view to arbitrate an amicable position between long-standing rivals India and Pakistan. In this way the film enters into a public discussion about the enmity and possible friendship between India and Pakistan that resounds throughout the South Asian diaspora too. Moreover, whilst *Main Hoon Na* is not set specifically between India and one of its diasporas—an anonymous urban city and predominantly Darjeeling are the two frames of reference wherein the film is set—the film's mise en scène deliberately depicts a look and feel of an urban India that is amalgamated with references from the diaspora. The location scenes at the college campus in Darjeeling are especially telling here as the costumes and performances of the bodies of Ram, Lucky, Sanjana and Miss Chandini, are all intelligible as emerging from and quoting the diasporic-infused college sets from earlier film like *Kuch Kuch Hota Hai*, *Mohabbatein* and *Kabhi Kushi Kabhie Gham*. Here characters wear attire and perform sociality in the happy-cum-comedic days of being at college that is a colourful mix of East and West—ethnic chic, Levis, retro-seventies garb, modern gadgets and transnational consumer goods such as Apple laptops and Pepsi beverages. Body postures and movements are confident and constantly on the go whether students are on the track field, attending classes, or singing and dancing at the American-style prom night reminicent of the sixties. The language spoken throughout the student campus is Hinglish, a hybrid and cosmopolitan mixture of Hindi, English and urban American slang, so that phrases such as 'whassup' and 'say what?' sit comfortably alongside filmi Hindi. It appears that these students typify the transitory and mobile features of urban India and the diaspora as informing each other through oscillating cultural sensibilities, dress codes, linguistic vernaculars and consumer durables. What the overall mise en scène and narrative impetus of *Main Hoon*

Na demonstrates, then, is that post-*DDLJ* and Shahrukh Khan's emergence as the premier urban/diasporic Indian figure in global post-nineties Hindi cinema, and even when an urban film is not set immediately in the diaspora or is about the homeland and diaspora, elements of the two are strategically invoked in the diegesis that aim to appeal to both constituencies simultaneously for profit and pleasure at the global Bollywood box office.

Figure 3.3: Ram (Shahrukh Khan) and Miss Chandni (Sushmita Sen) dance at the Indian-American style prom night in *Main Hoon Na*

Shahrukh's individual body—literally and metaphorically—is further interesting in an analysis of the performance of urban/diasporic Indian identity. The idea of the social as embodied through actual human subjects, both in a material and metaphorical sense of the body, now has a growing literature in the social sciences and in contemporary sociology in particular (Shilling 1993; Turner 1992). The body also becomes an increasingly metaphorical component in the organisation of modern social systems wherein the well-being of the nation is often illustrated through political and popular discourses to do with the functioning of a healthy or dysfunctional body politic (Baty 1995). The individual body of the star, and often the male star, in Hindi cinema has long been a trope for wider socio-cultural, economic and political aspirations, anxieties and comment. For example, the body of actor and star Amitabh Bachchan has been discussed elsewhere as providing a trope upon which the trials, tribulations and fantasies of the lower classes in India were played out in the seventies and eighties (Mishra 2002: Chapter 5; Sharma 1993). It is through the physical and symbolic body of Shahrukh Khan, standing at an average 5' 9" and of slim stature, that particular kinds of performances are enunciated that come to signify certain kinds of urban Indian and diasporic possibilities. We have already noted that Shahrukh Khan is the current esteemed global ambassador of Bollywood cinema through his dress and performance that mediate homeland, diasporic and transnational sensibilities. In addition he is an important player in the film industry who through product placements, production deals, and the setting up of his own media company, espouses an ideal towards increased upward mobility and opportunity for wealth and leisure accumulation as a sign of an aspirational commodified lifestyle for both urban and diasporic India. The articulation of urban and diasporic India vying for a comfortable and upwardly mobile lifestyle is often striven towards amidst melo-dramatic trials and a climactic resolve in which the body is often challenged in extreme ways before the anxiety is relieved and the aspirational attained in Bollywood cinema. In *Main Hoon Na* the melodrama of the nation and the family are intertwined and put through a series of trials played out through the bodies of the protagonists.

As the film *Main Hoon Na* heightens towards an explosive action finale, the students are held hostage at the college campus by Raghavan and his men in a final attempt to halt Project *Milaap*, and Ram is challenged by Raghavan to a battle in which only one will emerge victorious. While Ram embarks on his showdown with Raghavan, his mother on the road to reconciliation with him asks for the safe return of her two sons: '*Ram, mujhe mere dono bete wahpas chaiyye*' (Ram, I want both my sons back). As Ram and Raghavan battle it out, fist to fist, images of the prisoners on both sides of India and Pakistan being released and reunited with their families are interspersed with the fight scene (see Figure 3.4).

This climactic fight sequence between Ram and Raghavan is also indicative of another coming of age of Bollywood cinema under the aegis of globalisation. The fight is highly choreographed involving the

Figure 3.4: Fighting personal and national battles: Ram (Shahrukh Khan) combats with Raghavan (Sunil Shetty) in their final showdown as prisoners are released on either side of the Indo-Pak border

two actors, two martial arts stunt doubles from Bangkok,[7] the use of black-wire sequencing, and freeze time and digital technology post-*Matrix*. The culmination of these factors produce an on-screen action event of just under five minutes that seems much longer, akin to the heroic and lengthy battles between Ram and Ravan from the story of the Ramayana, due to the intensity of the sequence and the switching between the use of sharp, slow and fast-paced transitionary editing via digital technology. Digital technology in Bollywood cinema has been increasingly used since the late nineties (Gopalan 2002: 182–83), and digital intervention in the filmic medium has invoked a reconsideration of the ways in which diegetic time frames and actual audience time frames coalesce and diverge, producing an experience and sensation of immediacy and other worldliness simultaneously (Prince 2004). *Main Hoon Na* flaunts these developments, especially in its numerous action sequences, partly due to the large budget accorded to the film (approximately Rs 24.7 crore or Rs 247 million),[8] and partly by incorporating these technological moves as central to the diegetic narrative and character development as well. Shahrukh Khan is not only cast, yet again, as the prime urban/diasporic protagonist, he is also accorded a central status as a modern Indian Army soldier. In fact, as is acknowledged in the film dialogues, he is the best the army has to offer. Thus, Shahrukh Khan's/Ram's action sequences and his retort to his enemies have to be displayed at their ultimate best—a post-millennium Hindi cinema masala hero whose action is at par with his Hong Kong and Hollywood counterparts, using the technology advanced by Hong Kong and Hollywood cinemas initially, and then culturally translated in the specific idiom of Bollywood's mythic, religious, socio-political and everyday battles on screen. Ram and Raghavan, both before and after this battle finale, exchange dialogues directly referencing their namesakes from the original religious text as a referent to their own stand-off. Ram's body is battered and bloodied, as is expected of the action hero, conveying not only physical embellishes but also symbolic body politic bruises of internal struggles that need to be wrought with and overcome in an effort towards the peace process with Pakistan. The culmination of this bloody and explosive finale (Ram literally has to escape by running off an exploding roof and leaping on to a helicopter in order to survive) raises the stakes in the action capabilities of Hindi cinema. These possibilities, aided with developments in cinematic technology, further advance Bollywood cinema's foray into digital technology that translate into potential readings about the urban/ diasporic Indian as achieving ultimate masala goals—resolving melodramatic trials, overcoming personal and physical struggles, executing song and dance sequences excellently, mediating a rela-tionship between long-standing religious texts and globalisation—all performed through the agile human body as a literal and symbolic referent through which projects of selfhood are projected on screen. Shahrukh Khan is part of and performs these various enactments as possibilities rendered by Bollywood cinema that simultaneously offers audiences ideologies as well as new understandings and becomings. He is the epitomy of the 'now' of global Bollywood's cinematic assemblage.

4

Bollywood Cinema Going in New York City

This chapter draws on theoretical and interdisciplinary developments in film studies (metaphors of the body and skin, haptic codes in the cinematic experience, and Indian rasa theory), urban and cultural geography (the location of places and the theorising of spaces as informing subjectivity formation), and in sociology and cultural studies (diaspora and globalisation) to situate and offer an exploration of diasporic South Asian identity formation vis-à-vis Bollywood cinema going at two sites in New York City, USA. What is suggested is a complexifying of the sensations of the Bollywood cinematic assemblages that are consumed and incorporated in the cultural geographies and urban bodies of Bollywood's diasporic audiences in Jackson Heights in the borough of Queens, and in Times Square in the district of Manhattan. The chapter uses fieldwork notes of watching the same Bollywood film, *Koi... Mil Gaya* (I Have Met Someone, dir. Rakesh Roshan, 2003), at these two different locations during the summer of 2003 to elaborate on the aforementioned theoretical work.[1]

The chapter maps out some of the socio-cultural sensations of popular Hindi cinema in their moment of globalisation. The experience of Bollywood cinema going in Jackson Heights and in Times Square is situated and compared within the context of a globalising cinema, whose apparatus, financial structure, narrative strategies, and bodily technologies are being dismantled and restructured. The chapter ends with a consideration of two influential theories for understanding the effects of these transformations in the embodied life of the sensations of Bollywood: haptic visuality and rasa aesthetics.

HAPTIC I: JACKSON HEIGHTS

Take a ride on the W Train into Queens from 42nd St. Our stop is at 74th St. and Roosevelt Ave, Jackson Heights. We descend into an immigrant carnival, a post-9/11 surveillance nightmare, a migrant fantasy, mundane working-class reality, all in a three-mile radius.[2] Trains passing overhead, ongoing city construction, this is a place being remade, commuter traffic cutting off the flows of pedestrians. We make our way on to 74th St., crossing 37th Rd. Bustling Latino and South Asian grocery stores, with juicy mangoes on sale outside, glittering jewellery on display in store fronts, white mannequins draped in the latest saris, the aroma of masala-smothered chaat direct our attention to diners and dhabas, the latest South Asian books and magazines on sale next to incense, digestion medicine, and religious amulets and holy statues, beauty parlours inviting you to look your best, the beats and rhythms of a range of South Asian music genres blaring out on to the street from speakers in music and video stores. On bus stop walls, pay phones and utility poles, flyers for the latest Bollywood concert in New Jersey hang next to reminders for the next immigrant rights, anti-racist or de-detention rally in the neighbourhood. The world at this crossroads brings together immigrant histories, the forging of community spaces, post-9/11 racialised urban geographies, and the bodily desires and sensual commodities that work in relation to these formations.

Jackson Heights provides us with a preliminary thesis on the kinds of transformations of global Bollywood. First, we must mark a profound acceleration in the speed of commercial Bombay cinema (or Bollywood) today. We return to this in a moment, but clearly these speeds, and their differential axes and rhythms, are discernible in the contrast between Bollywood at Loews Theatre in Times Square (Manhattan) and Eagle Theatre in Jackson Heights (Queens). A globalising economic and cultural matrix for Bollywood is operative in both, but the speeds and their intensities differ markedly. First, the resonances of the local, or, better, the continuing salience of the spatiality of the 'neighbourhood' in Jackson Heights marks it as a space that has been configured by the patterns of migration, rather than one formed through the circuits of tourism (as in Times Square). With a non-white population fast approaching 60 per cent of a multicultural whole, Queens is one of the most diverse places in America. More specifically in Jackson Heights, Asians make up over 30 per cent of the population, with South Asians accounting for well over a third of the Asian community. As one New York-based tourist website put it:

> Jackson Heights is different [from other tourist areas in New York]. Seventy-fourth Street between Roosevelt Avenue and 37th Avenue and the surrounding blocks are the heart of a South Asian neighbourhood. Indians, Bangladeshis, and Pakistanis call this area home, and come here to shop and eat. It's the place for some of the highest quality Indian food in New York City; South Asian jewellery, clothes, and music; Bollywood films; and plain old people-watching. This is a great neighbourhood for strolling and taking it all in.[3]

Jackson Heights is known not only throughout America, but increasingly throughout the world because of satellite TV. B4U and Sony Entertainment TV, two major satellite channels, regularly feature commercials for merchants, usually jewellers, from this South Asian community. In many ways it is thought of as the heart of the South Asian community in New York. Jackson Heights has had a complex history as a 'get-away' spot from Manhattan. In the twenties and thirties Jackson Heights became a haven for gay and lesbian people working in Vaudeville, who were either unable or unwilling to live in Manhattan. Since the late sixties it has come to be a destination place for new Asian immigrants, who enter the US either through the sponsorship of a relative or on tourist or immigrant visas. These new immigrants join the swelling ranks of underpaid and overworked service-sector employees, whose meagre wages are split between themselves and their dependents back home.

Certainly, then, Jackson Heights is a neighbourhood, even as we might be wary of all the romanticism inherent in that word. Interestingly, this aura of Jackson Heights as romantic immigrant neighbourhood has been both celebrated and problematised in Bollywood films as well.[4]

Situated in the heart of Jackson Heights, is Eagle Theatre (see Figure 4.1). Formerly screening pornography films, Eagle now shows the latest Bollywood hits reinscribing the history of its own space by marketing itself as 'The House of Family Entertainment'.[5] In one sense this is true enough: overwhelmingly, it is families or social groups who form the interpretive units at Eagle, not individuals. The Eagle Theatre is owned by a Pakistani immigrant, although he has made it clear that he has no particular nationalist agenda. Formerly known as The Earle, it was built in the thirties, in a typical art deco style common for movie theatres of that era (an architectural style that itself translated the perceived speeds of modernity into a new arrangement of lines and curves and moulded concrete). The various owners of Eagle Theatre over the years have not modified its facade significantly, and even the light fixtures and panelling inside seem to have been left intact. Eagle is in the middle of an almost, always busy street (37th Rd.), situated next to a popular CD/DVD and video

Figure 4.1: The Eagle Theatre, Jackson Heights (personal photograph)

rental store, a phone card stand, and at the end of the block stands the popular Kabob King Cafe. There are four main national groups that frequent Eagle: Indians, Pakistanis, Bangladesis, and increasingly Nepalis (in fact, the Nepali community regularly screens its own films at Eagle).

How, then, do we approach the experience of viewing Bollywood films in Eagle Theatre? What marks this cinema in the minds of its patrons as a specifically *desi* space?[6]

First, there is a sense of a class memory that seems to live in the space, given off by the musty air of garam masala, paan juice, and cheap air freshener, the two tiers of the theatre, vaguely recalling the expensive dress circle (or balcony) and cheap stalls of Indian movie halls. It's a place where the staff work on very clear and well-established patterns of patronage, ethnic familiarity and solid business sense. One non-desi visitor put it thus:

> It's the kind of place that charges $8 for a ticket (which simply says, 'Keep This Coupon') but will discount the price so that the total enables the ticket guy to give back a large bill to the purchaser when he doesn't have enough small bills for change.[7]

In a way that is completely distinct from the experience of viewing at Loews Theatre, audiences in Jackson Heights mark and are marked by the diegetic space (by which both the space of viewing and the narrative space are alluded to here). Talking back to the screen, commenting on the narrative, hooting and hollering, euphoric greetings of familiar stars, talking to family members or friends, singing along, comforting a crying baby, eating a *roti* from Kabob King, and taking a much needed loo-break during the song-dance sequences—these are all normal and expected practices of viewing at Eagle, which can themselves be demarcated in terms of various determinations. For instance, consider gender normality (what women are expected to do, what they do, and what men can do and actually do): the interpretive-affective unit of viewership (the extended family, or social or kinship group) constitutes a vector of conjugal, domestic, familial gender regulations that impinge on women unequally. These regularities, however, are criss-crossed by disjunctive cultural formations (forms of hybridity) that allow for specific lines of flight, forms of agency, and new subjections. Thus, second generation *desi* women adopt forms of viewership that both enable them to claim a certain belonging to normalised gender, and yet in that very claim to assert a specifically tactical agency—without necessarily thinking in terms of resistance or complicity. Many of the women we spoke with, for instance, insisted that going to the movies was a way of connecting to family and culture while simultaneously asserting a stylised nostalgia through which they established this connection (the craze for bhangra clubbing among this generation of desis could be understood through this double movement). What is being suggested here is that this is a specifically gendered negotiation. Moreover, ethnic, religious, caste and class access to the normative subjectivity of the active viewer of Bollywood entails a detailed mapping of the specific diagram of power, space, narrative, subjectivity and history that Eagle Theatre puts into play. Although a more complete mapping is beyond the scope of this chapter, the argument being put forward is that Eagle Theatre is a cinematic assemblage of such vectors of affect, intensity, technology, subjection, discourse, and space.

We have a sense of the accelerations which constitute this filmic experience: the rhythm of viewing in Eagle has a tempo that is formed and interrupted by all the competing economies of the immigrant business community in Jackson Heights—food vendors who give flavour to filmic images, while the video store next door provides music tapes, CDs and DVDs (both can be purchased before or after the showing); three or four groups of viewers just stepping off the late-running MTA Bus file in, looking for seats, blocking your view of the screen, but no one worries because there is an advertisement on screen for a computer training institute which is followed by another ad for Resham Silk, a sari store. Resham Silk offers the finest silks and saris, and Access Computer Training, 10 per cent Early Bird Discounts and H-1 visas.[8] Another ad announces the opening of a concert film of famed Sufi Qawwal, Nusrat Fateh Ali Khan.

With this very schematic portrait of Eagle Theatre and Jackson Heights in mind, let us return to the first thesis concerning the accelerations of Bollywood. The speed of Bollywood is increasing for two interrelated reasons: first, because the media-lines of dissemination are proliferating; Bollywood can be found in the most unexpected places of the world, from Kenya to Iran, to Trinidad to Kansas. Each site is a singularity, and yet multiply connected to the globalising circuits of exchange, consumption and viewing that define contemporary Mumbai cinema's regimes of bodily pleasure. Further, Indian production houses were only recently granted industry status by the government in 1998, thereby opening up new avenues of legitimate, or non-'black' financial underwriting (see Chapter 6). Thus new economic models for a globalising film industry are spurring proliferation and profusion of these media-lines: 20th Century Fox co-produced the recent Partition-era social drama *Pinjar* (Cage, dir. C.P. Dwivedi, 2003). The cross-merchandising pleasures on sale at the new Bollywood multiplexes (both in India and in the diaspora) are mapping more and more territories for ever more speedy dissemination.

The second reason for the rapid spread of Bollywood is the increase in the types of media: digital, satellite, air, print, Internet, radio, optical cables, digital subscriber lines (or DSL), and telephone. For instance, it is now possible to subscribe to any one of a number of Bollywood channels through Dishnet Satellite TV and simultaneously be put in touch with, via the Internet, hundreds of Bollywood websites. In another example, one local Indian grocery store in Tallahassee, Florida, had the latest hit *Kal Ho Naa Ho* (Tommorow May Never Come, dir. Nikhil Advani, 2003) in the week of its cinema release. Two reasons, then, both essentially related to the proliferation of media-lines. These explanations offer new sites and new technologies that result in new media commodities, and indeed new possibilities for commodifying the sensations of Bollywood. It should be noted further that both these increases in media speeds are discernible at the level of the diegesis: narratives are speeding up, there are less songs, shorter average shot duration, long- to medium-range shots enabling quicker and more economical editing. Almost all of Ram Gopal Varma's films from *Satya* (Truth, 1998) onwards would fit this characterisation. However, even more traditionally lavish directors such as Raj Kumar Santoshi have moved toward this aesthetic—for instance, his recent film *Khakee* (Police Uniform, 2004).

But, it must be further qualified what kinds of experiences that are being made available through this speeding up of Bollywood. We could begin by noting that a pirated copy of *Kal Ho Naa Ho* that we saw was very poor, and this in turn implies something about the way in which these speeds are lived, or better, that the media-lines of connectivity (in this case pirated DVDs) are differentially ordered in relation to a privileged cosmopolitan and high-technology Bollywood space. This privileged cosmopolitan space no longer refers to a fixed and essential nation state: rather, commercial Hindi cinema has reterritorialised the nation in the diaspora. But the point here is that specific forms of urban life with their privileged sites of performance focus on new technologies as both signs and vehicles of globalisation. For instance, the DVD boom for Bollywood has meant not only more profits, more pirating and more regulations, but it also presents this cinema with the possibility of a new look, a multifaceted translatability as a portable media commodity.

In a sense, the acceleration of this cosmopolitan commodity—the globalised Hindi film—has produced many skins as it were, many surfaces, plug-ins, and amplitudes in Jackson Heights. Film literally touches just about every aspect of immigrant South Asian life. Hindi cinema is, in other words, a haptic medium. In thinking about commercial Hindi cinema as a haptic media event the work of both Gilles Deleuze and Laura Marks is discussed here. In his elaboration of Francis Bacon's Logic of Sensation, Deleuze defines haptic space (from the Greek verb apto which means to touch) as a space in which there is no longer a hand-eye subordination in either direction. It implies a type of seeing distinct from the optical, a close-up viewing in which the sense of sight behaves just like the sense of touch.[9]

Extending and transforming this experience of vision through our memory of other senses (touch only being one of them), Laura Marks argues that the skin of a film 'offers a metaphor to emphasize the way film signifies through its materiality, through a contact between perceiver and object represented' (Marks 2000). To think of film as a skin acknowledges the effect of a work circulating among different audiences, all of which mark it with their presence. 'Film (and video) may be thought of as impressionable and conductive, like skin. I want to emphasize the tactile and contagious quality of cinema as something we viewers brush up against like another body' (ibid.: xii). These provocative suggestions open new lines of thought for Bollywood criticism by returning us to one of the oldest forms of understanding the pleasures of the body: rasa theory.[10]

As many critics have noted before, Bharat-munia's sixth century Natya shastra provides South Asians with a ready matrix with which to experience not only Bollywood but a good samosa as well.[11] As Richard Schechner in a provocative and programmatic article argues, rasa also means 'juice', the stuff that conveys the flavour, the medium of tasting. The juices of eating originate both in the food and from the body. Saliva not only moistens food, it distributes flavours. Rasa is sensuous, proximate, experiential. Rasa is aromatic.

Rasa fills space, joining the outside to the inside. Food is actively taken into the body, becomes part of the body, works from the inside. What was outside is transformed into what is inside. An aesthetic founded on rasa is fundamentally different than one founded on the 'theatron, the rationally ordered, analytically distanced panoptic' (Schechner 2001: 29). If not panoptic, rasa could certainly be thought of as haptic (indeed what is being argued here is that rasa could be thought of as the haptic codes of Bollywood). But further problems arise when we consider rasa theory as not only an aesthetic theory but a divine experience (which is what makes the Natya shastra a shastra, or divine text, after all). This would immediately imply a culturally specific divine: Brahmanical elite discourse masquerading as the universal truth of beauty. Consider this translation from verses 1–20 of Chapter One, 'The Origin of Natya [Drama]':

> 'Long, long, very long ago,' said Bharata, 'People of this world of pain and pleasure, goaded by greed and avarice, and jealousy and anger, took to uncivilized (lit.: gramya=vulgar) ways of life. [The world] was then inhabited by gods, demons, yaksa-s, raksasa-s, naga-s, and gandharva-s. Various lords were ruling. It was the gods among them who, led by Mahendra, approached God Brahma and requested him (thus): 'Please give us something which would not only teach us but be pleasing both to eyes and ears. [True] the Vedas are there but [some like] the Sudras ["lower castes"] are prohibited from listening to [learning from] them. Why not create for us a fifth Veda which would be accessible to all the varna-s (castes)?' (Rangacharya 1996:1)

Clearly, we could understand this birth of drama from the point of view of social struggle: in an effort to curb lower-caste vulgarity, an aesthetic pedagogy, that is a discursive practice of the civilised body, was put in place.[12] Historically, however, this reading of rasa discourse as elite Brahmanic pedagogy is complicated by the fact that the Natya shastra was the only one of the Vedas that was to be enjoyed by all castes; moreover, when the text says that the sons of Bharata [the purported author of the Natya shastra] ridiculed the sages and were therefore cursed to be born Sudras, one historical meaning of this is that drama was the profession of the 'lower' castes, or Dalits.[13] If the Natya shastra, then, could be thought of in our contemporary terms as the most 'democratic' of Vedas, one whose history bears the marks of caste struggles and the memory of Dalit resistance to Brahman hegemony, we would like to think of rasa not as an abstract theory of sensual pleasure but as a coded discipline marked by what Laura Marks terms a kind of contagion of the skin of film. The experience of Bollywood both on the screen and in the space of viewing has been marked by contagions—bodily, cultural and ideological, and sensual. In colonial and post-colonial India, the Chief Medical Officer of the State is the personage who has administered permits to 'Talkies'. The conceptual framework of the haptic film allows us to map the media-event of Bollywood as an assemblage of impressionable and conductive surfaces. Bollywood as a 'contact zone' (Mary Pratt's felicitous phrase; see Pratt 1992) through and in which bodies, sensations, capital, sexualities, races, technologies and desires rub up against each other, producing differing and differential rhythms, speeds, juices (or rasas), intensities, technologies, combinations, codes, possibilities, and even languages. Haptic Bollywood would be that form of film culture that operates through a commodified sensorium, one that produces new possibilities of sensations (new contagious juices), even as the novelty of the experiences is value-added, in and for the codes of a globalising Bollywood.

HAPTIC II: BOLLYWOOD IN TIMES SQUARE

We are, first, in the midst of pure movement. The flows are intense in all directions, multiple voltages of machinic energy, halts, distractions and divergences, all occurring in different directions. Here we experience flows criss-crossed by other flows, lines of desire, lights intercepting lights, flowing into both haptic and perspectival images, flowing out through commodity exchanges, movements of uptown-downtown yellow cabs (with mostly South Asian drivers), the flows of market information on electronic ticker tape. The vertical integration of the Hollywood film industry early in the twentieth century is mirrored today in the vertical visual organisation of the spectacle at 'the Crossroads of the World'. From all sides, media images climb up towards the sky, multiple vistas open up to the viewer–tourist. A permanent carnival exists with sideshows at every corner. Throughout this space a range of images are up for sale: on the streaming marquees, on the video screens, on the sidewalk; images of the New York landscape, of this world famous space and of star personalities. You can have your face drawn by the (mostly East Asian) artists and join Al Pacino in the panoply of stars for sale. There exist economies within economies: East Asian artists vie with each other to do the next drawing, an African-American photographer (with his own colour printer and glossy paper) offering instant photos, street theatre artists miming silver statues. These are subjects that are plugged into and at the same time excluded from the spectacle of corporate media that forms and reforms before our wondering eyes. This is Times Square in New York City (see Figure 4.2).

In what ways, then, does the experience of Bollywood at the Loews Theatre in Times Square contribute to our formulation of considering commercial Hindi cinema as haptic media? As a way of addressing this question and to elaborate further on the similarities and

Figure 4.2: Haptic images and social flows in Times Square, New York City (personal photograph)

differences between the two Bollywood cinema going sites in New York we turn to our participant observations[14] and fieldwork notes of viewing *Koi... Mil Gaya* at Loews Theatre (see Figure 4.3) and compare these with our viewing experience of the same film at Eagle Theatre.

Figure 4.3: The outside of the Loews Theatre in Times Square situated in the Virgin Megastore (personal photograph)

It is a warm and humid early evening in August. We wind our way through the crowds in Times Square. Unlike Jackson Heights, we do not notice many other South Asians going to Loews—not until we get there. The sidewalk is crammed with people, hawkers and showmen; we move on quickly, getting to the Virgin Megastore. Immediately, as we enter, we are greeted with a gust of arctic air conditioning and a wall covered with DVDs and CDs; we acclimatise ourselves in the lobby of Virgin, as a panoptic DJ tower (whose box while always empty, never seems to be without a CD spinning away) stares over us. We take the escalator down, past the mezzanine, into the very depths of the building; behind the escalator is the entrance to Loews Theatre, where a line has already formed.

Ten minutes to show time we spot a few South Asians in the queue, dressed in their Manhattan best. Loews is a discount multiplex cinema with its mainstream Hollywood films advertised at $4.95 thereby attracting a mixed audience in terms of race and class. However, the ticket price for each Bollywood showing is $10. Loews hires the prints of Bollywood films for a one-off fee and hence the 'double-the-price' for its viewing is to reflect a commercial strategy on Loews' part to recuperate its cost and any profits as quickly as possible. Whereas class is almost a non-issue in terms of the audience composition for screenings of Hollywood movies, we soon realise that it is social class that separates Bollywood audiences in Times Square and in Jackson Heights: the ability to afford the ticket and the mode of dress that goes with the evening out is definitely a middle-class privilege.

We buy our tickets from a young African American man with an older West Indian female colleague standing behind him in the ticket booth. We pay with a credit card, because unlike Eagle Lowes is not primarily a cash economy. It is based fundamentally on the great American debt: enjoy now, pay later or forever.

We enter a corridor directing us towards the theatre, to our right there are some arcade video games and seating but no one is waiting there now: it appears that people have moved on to get their seats. We take an escalator to go down, a Filipina woman tears our tickets, we descend another level (our fourth level down). As we get off the escalators we see the 'concession' stand open for business where a one litre bottle of water costs $3.50 (some concession). We buy snacks from the young black Latino behind the counter and move toward the theatre. A young African American man stands at the ready to check out torn ticket stubs and then to let us through into the theatre hall. The process of entering the building via the Virgin Megastore right down to purchasing our tickets and making our way to the cinema auditorium appears to have taken at least three or four minutes. In that short space of time, as patrons making our way into the cinema, we partake in being surveyed (the security cameras are always tacitly working overhead) and been deemed legitimate to make our way further into the dream palace (our ticket stubs having been checked twice). The maze of escalators, corridors and expensive food booths implicitly function as part of the Loews Theatre's assemblage which wants us to believe that the fantasy of images in which we are about to enter is 'worth it' for the extra price that we are paying.

We move into the darkened hall. It is comprised of a sloping seating arrangement. Most of the South Asians have already occupied the 'balcony' rows. We take side row seats. The movie *Koi... Mil Gaya* starts: A spaceship lands in north India. A little blue alien is accidentally left behind by his fellow aliens. A magical adventure begins as a young man, Rohit (Hrithik Roshan), with the mental age of a 10-year-old, meets and befriends this little blue creature, *Jaadoo* (Magic) (see Figure 4.4). The alien learns what it means to be human and the young man becomes a man. Genres collide as Hindi romance-melodrama meets sci-fi, wherein boy (Rohit) meets girl (Nisha played by Preity Zinta), man becomes (super)hero, and narratives of love and friendship mix seamlessly together.

Three hours later we follow the crowd out. One of us was able to talk to a group of viewers, a family, who had come from New Jersey. They all agreed it was too long, and that Hrithik Roshan, the film's male lead, had done a fantastic job. This was not their first time at

Figure 4.4: Rohit (Hrithik Roshan) and Nisha (Preity Zinta) make friends with the little blue alien Jaadoo in *Koi... Mil Gaya*

Loews and they had been here before. It confirmed a hypothesis of ours that the majority of viewers for the Times Square venue of Bollywood had in fact come from Brooklyn, New Jersey and Manhattan, and that unlike their co-patrons who pay half for entry into Hollywood films, and unlike their co-diasporics in Queens, these viewers are overwhelmingly middle-class professionals.

We manoeuvre our way back up to the ground floor of the Virgin Megastore and outside on to the bustling sidewalks of Time Square. We are surrounded by an aura of different images all lit-up and exaggerated against the evening night. We talk on the metro ride home trying to grasp the social act that had just unfolded before us, and that we also took part in.

Our sense is that much of the audience response to the film at Loews was very similar to that of Eagle. Indeed, the audience at Loews was just as active if not more than the one at Eagle. Whilst there is a difference in terms of the audience composition at these two venues in terms of social class, it does not follow from our observations that the audience interaction in the darkness of the two auditoriums is starkly different as a result of class. Thus, interpreting audience behaviour in this instance as based around an idea of being initiated according to social class is difficult to sustain. Moreover, there was a profound overlap in terms of the precise moments that elicited laughter (for instance, the appearance of actor Johnny Lever in an obligatory comic role), sighs, camaraderie, hushed expectation, wows, and so on. In other words, in both auditorium experiences one can see how sensation is produced through the strategic integration of differently accented narrative segments; thus we have the joke sketch, the romance, the tragedy, the social critique, the return-of-the-diasporic, the completion of the father through the son motif, the religious track, the good guy versus the bad guy segmentation— all embedded in *Koi… Mil Gaya*. All these segments are given relative force through the soundtrack, the background score, the cinematography, montage, the mise en scène, and the camera action. These sensations that can be read through the body are affects–effects embedded in the 'interruptive narrative';[15] the cinematic assemblage is this passage from narrative to sensation and back. There is no point of origin or line of development but rather a spiralling relationship, moving in directions yet unknown and in ways yet to be fully classified. Indeed, it is in this relationship between affect and the sensational narratives of commercial Hindi cinema that the essential openness of this form of cultural production can be located. This cinema maintains a decentered process of production in so many ways: there are multiple sources for the narrative—the Ramayana, South Asian history, the Mughal court, the *zanaana* or women's public sphere, the non-nuclear family, Hollywood, and nationalist mythologisations—which are all simultaneously possible sources of meaning. And the non-unitary, the non-linear and non-subjective process of producing, framing, setting, shooting and editing form alternate sites of authority, producing a collective text.[16]

Perhaps the most clear example of the essential openness of this cinema is not in the story itself but in the economies of affect–effect set in play at the specific cinematic assemblages. What is being suggested here then, is that if audience interaction is similar in the cinema halls at these two different sites in one city what marks and sets them apart, drawing from our observations, is the cultural geographies in which these specific cinematic assemblages are located and work. In other words, although a set script—that encompasses the components of narrative, mise en scène, etc.— helps to determine the normative affects–effects to be elicited, it is the assemblage that gives expression to this affective matter, configuring it through its own specificity. Thus, it is possible to argue here that the role of Bollywood star, Hrithik Roshan, in *Koi... Mil Gaya* can be understood in similar and different, yet related ways at these two cinematic assemblages in New York. At Eagle, if the predominant interpretive unit of this film is the family, then a reading of the film is possible by this audience along lines which embrace Hrithik Roshan as one of their Bollywood stars in the diasporic space of Jackson Heights and also which embrace Hrithik Roshan as star son directed by his father Rakesh Roshan, who also acts briefly in the film, as understood amidst articulations of fan culture and also of the representation of South Asian family life through the nuances of Bollywood cinema.[17] At the Loews Theatre this interpretation is also viable. Additionally, the star persona and representation of Hrithik Roshan is further articulated amidst the giant hoardings of Hollywood stars, US TV celebrities and global consumer ads that vie for your attention in the immediate vicinity and as part of the Loews assemblage. Here, Hrithik Roshan, the Loews' Bollywood audience and their on- and off-screen fantasies and aspirations, mediated through the social act of cinema going to see *Koi... Mil Gaya*, also become part of the cinematic assemblage in Times Square.[18]

We think about Bollywood cinema being offered in the midst of the flows of Times Square. Here, the commodification and reterritorialisation of Bollywood narratives takes place in the margins of a carnival of multinational and corporate desire. Times Square is a physical and social matrix of flows—of people, of traffic, of electronic communication, of images and capital shifting in all directions. It is a 'crossroads' where corporate culture and ghetto cultures appear to meet on the large hoardings and are commodified and made safe for a predominantly white and upwardly mobile class—one does not have to look far to notice the stock market shares and global news being updated every minute. Contemporary Times Square is manufactured as the absolute present—it appears that it has no past and one seldom has time to think about the future as the here and now is what appears to matter. The next line of the electronic ticker tape carrying financial information is presented not as something new, but just the next line. Time Square is the epitome of modern urban America's image of itself to itself; it presents the present and manages the anxiety of the future.[19]

Equally, just as desire is on offer and produced through the multiplicity of images and technologies at the crossroads of the world, Times Square is also one of the most surveyed and guarded places in the US, not just after 9/11 but also historically. The middle- and upwardly mobile-class pleasures, desires and whitewashing of this geographical space are not accidental but have been sought after and actively encouraged by a select, powerful few. Neil Smith has demonstrated how the gentrification of Manhattan and Times Square in particular has been part of a 'vicious revanchism' under the then leadership of Mayor Rudy Giuliani from the mid-ninties onwards (Smith 1998: 1). 'Revanchism blends revenge with social reaction' and the police and other municipal authorities under 'Giuliani time' aimed to reclaim the public spaces of New York that were considered to be stolen from the white middle classes by vagrants and minorities (ibid.: 1–4). As a result, police brutality was on the up in the city under the infamous programme of 'zero tolerance', and central areas were cleared of homeless people and pornography stores—the outer borough areas became the dumping ground. All this to make way for 'the suburbanisation of the city' and the consolidation of the 'multi-billion dollar Disney mother colony' in Times Square where geographies of material culture, real estate capital and revanchism seem perfectly synchronised (ibid.: 8–14).[20] It appears that Giuliani's successor, Michael Bloomberg, is just as eager to further suburbanise and gentrify central areas of New York.[21]

In contrast, as has been argued above, there is the cinematic assemblage of Eagle Cinema, also in New York (but decidedly not in the 'City'), offering Bollywood films in the context of a different kind of cultural geography. Here, Eagles' diasporisation and familiarising of both the narratives of the films and the spaces of their viewing takes place through processes of embedding the culture of film within broader immigrant and racialised entrepreneurial cultures, geographies and economies. So what conclusions are possible from this initial set of experiences of the sensations of popular Hindi cinema in their moment of globalisation?

CONCLUSION

Deleuze once said that colour

is in the body, sensation is in the body, and not in the air. Sensation is what is painted. What is painted on the canvas is the body, not insofar as it is represented as an object, but insofar as it is experienced as sustaining this sensation.[22]

The notion of sensation in Deleuze is about the mobilisation of the body, beyond the brain and into the muscles through the actual nervous system. Beyond meaningful representations, sensation is that which enables creation to become an event of—through and in—the body. But what triggers sensation? Is sensation before discourse, like the Lacanian imaginary, or is sensation a singularity, each sensation in its own specificity each time? The sense that is being put forward here is that sensation or affect is both outside of history and the very precondition of it, like the horizon of history's becoming other: the Untimely.

Becoming isn't part of history; history amounts only [to] the set of preconditions, however recent, that one leaves behind in order to 'become,' that is, to create something new. This is precisely what Nietzsche calls the Untimely (Deleuze 1995: 171).

What is it that causes a sensation to vibrate beyond the boundaries of the proper (a juridical realm), propriety (a moral limit) and property (a marker of possession)? In response what has been explored here is the assemblage—the putting into play a multiplicity of connections, speeds and apparatuses. On the right side of propriety, argues Deleuze, is the sensational.

> In any case, Bacon has always tried to eliminate the 'sensational', that is, the primary figuration of that which provokes a violent sensation. This is the meaning of the formula, 'I wanted to paint the scream more than the horror.' ... Thus neutralized, the horror is multiplied because it is inferred from the scream, and not the reverse. And certainly it is not easy to renounce the horror, or the primary figuration (Smith 2003: 34).

In contrast, sensation and its violence are opposed to 'the violence of the represented (the sensational, the cliché)' (ibid.); sensation acts directly on the nervous system, 'which is of the flesh, whereas abstract form is addressed to the head and acts through the intermediary of the brain, which is closer to the bone' (ibid.: 31). Moreover, each sensation exists

> at diverse levels, in different orders, or in different domains. This means that there are not sensations of different orders, but different orders of one and the same sensation. It is the nature of sensation to envelop a constitutive difference of level, a plurality of constituting domains (ibid.: 33).

Hence the 'accumulation' of sensation. It is in the sensation that the subject becomes and something happens through the sensation.

What is this becoming and what is this event in contemporary Hindi film culture? Here we must speak of many faces. Because already we see that if we are to speak of the sensations of Bollywood, rather than merely the sensational (represented) in this cinema, we must speak of multiplicities, a cinematic assemblage. In our fieldwork, we have so far focused on two differently accelerating assemblages: The Square where Time stands still, an assemblage whose face is turned toward the Disney World of a globalised economy that melds sensations, affects, intensities in the wonders of transnational commodities. These commodities, produced by clearly segmented working populations, are themselves readily translated by various technologies of desire—the dance club, the movie theatre, the car stereo, the laptop: contemporary Bollywood cinema also aspires to attain such commodities. And the other assemblage which negotiates the contemporary post-9/11 moment by multiplying its face—seeking integration (into scripts of America, into new immigrant economies, into globalised circuits of exchange, services and labour) and demanding recognition of radical differences (of race, region, religion and neighbourhood, for instance). If this cinema functions through the haptic, the touch of sight, this would not be the name of the universal sensation of Bollywood, only one of its levels. If the haptic is one of the levels of sensations of Hindi cinema, its figure is enabled by a line of flight from the violence of these faces, a zigzag into the post-colonial 'pathic': 'Between a color, a taste, a touch, a smell, a noise, a weight, there would be an existential communication that would constitute the 'pathic' (non-representative) moment of the sensation' (Smith 2003: 37).

All of the above, then, implies something more about the diagram of Hindi film criticism. Too long has a certain criticism, in the name of the people, claimed to show them the way towards full humanity by transforming itself into a pedagogy of revolutionary pleasure; a pleasure attainable through an analysis, predominantly of the narrative and representation per se of Bollywood cinema. Rarely, has it posed the much simpler, but far more difficult question: how does it work and what is its diagram of power? And this is where questions of representation and key motifs in popular Hindi cinema (of race, class, gender, religion, etc.) can be considered through a sociological imagination (i.e., questioning the taken-for-granted nature about these representations) and developed further through a wider and contextual engagement with its routes, apparatuses of desire and cultural production in globalisation. What we see, then, both in our provisional maps of two differently constituted cinematic assemblages and in our experiences of affect in these desiring machines is the subject called into becoming by these multiplicities, punctuated by nodes (pedagogies of desire, which Hindi film criticism unwittingly repeats and displaces), traversed by a vector (a pure force of a sensational appropriation), and gravitated toward an Object (the always red-hot aspirational commodity). That vector of the Object whose nodes are training grounds for the subject's molar and dominant becomings (cosmopolitan consumer, Indian immigrant, American citizen, Woman-Man, or chic Other) is of course itself traversed with other vectors (space, speed, temporality, taste, light, rhythm, short- and long-term memory, affect)[23] and the lines of flight that they enable. A strategic mapping of these vectors, nodes and possible and actual becomings would be the aim of continuing this project further.

5

QUEER AS *DESIS*: SECRET
POLITICS OF GENDER AND
SEXUALITY IN BOLLYWOOD
FILMS IN DIASPORIC
URBAN ETHNOSCAPES

The international mass media talked about the summer of Bollywood in Britain in 2002. In particular, the month of May saw the celebration of Bollywood-inspired fashion and lifestyle accessories at the Selfridge's stores in the cities of London and Manchester over almost a month. There was mainstream coverage leading up to this event on the television and radio, in the press, the glossy magazines, and the Sunday newspaper supplements.[1] The following month Andrew Lloyd Weber's musical *Bombay Dreams* opened at London's Apollo Victoria Theatre in June. Around this time also, pop stars were using the aesthetics of Bollywood cinema to add an extra zest to their music, videos, style and popular iconography: Holly Vallance's track 'Kiss' is a case in point.

Numerous other examples could be listed from British popular culture as taking up the Bollywood interest which carried on into 2003: the British television series *Footballers Wives* and the British soap opera *Emmerdale Farm*, both aired on the ITV channel, consisted of Bollywood-inspired sets or sub-plots in which white characters were playing out their fantasies of the 'other'. High street fashion outlets such as Top Man, Top Shop and HandM were selling Bollywood-inspired clothes and accessories. Interestingly, the same style glossies (*Marie Clare, Cosmopolitan* and *Vanity Fair*) that were celebrating Bollywood in 2002 were claiming, by 2003, that the Bollywood fashion-fad had now passed and that their readers should move on. In this context, 'brown' was 'the new black' but Bollywood in Britain was being celebrated amidst orientalist and exotic sensibilities in the British mainstream rather than for its emergence as a serious addition to popular culture (Aftab 2002).[2]

On the one hand, then, Bollywood received widespread publicity and was noticed in 2002, certainly in the UK and more widely in the international arena. On the other hand, however, what needs to be noted is that it was the camp, kitsch and fun aspects of Bollywood as safe commodification that was overplayed in a lot of the images and written text that accompanied the celebration and appropriation of Hindi cinema in Britain over the last few years. Camp, kitsch and fun have always been part of Bollywood cinema but these were used in simplistic ways in these aforementioned examples that the mainstream cultural and entertainment industries focused on. The colourful and larger than life references from Bollywood cinema were used as commodified kitsch and were therefore trivialised in the mainstream appropriation of Bollywood, rather than also acknowledging the cultural politics that Bollywood's camp and kitsch might enable.

Related to this celebration, and interestingly only until a few years ago, Bollywood cinema was being ridiculed or marginalised in serious Western film scholarship. Bollywood has often been termed as a cinema of the masses, as trivial and everyday, something that the lower classes enjoy for basic pleasures.[3] This view of Bollywood was somewhat at odds in the actual commodification of Bollywood as a consumer experience, especially in the Selfridges store where loud and glittery aesthetic arrangements were used simply to sell goods and make a profit. For example, Bollywood film stars' designer bathrooms and bedrooms could be replicated in British homes for up to £15,000. Cushions and pillows were on sale from £40 up to £500 each. These are just two examples of the many high-priced items that were on sale. Clearly, this was a different kind of Bollywood mass audience (Asian and non-Asian) with a considerable amount of spending power that Selfridges was appealing to. The glitter, the colour, the music, the conversations, the fashion—all relating to popular Hindi cinema—were well intentioned, but what is being suggested here is that there was something not quite right about this particular celebration of Bollywood. The festivity espoused here was one where consumption was heralded as a privileged economic activity and the use of Bollywood as a cultural resource was underplayed, at best, if not missing altogether.

The point being made is that the camp and kitsch festivities around Bollywood in the summer months of 2002 were not just a construction of the Western cultural and entertainment industries but that they were drawing on, although in implicit ways, on the aesthetics and conventions of Bollywood cinema and its popular culture without wanting to be overwhelmed by the cultural politics of Bollywood's camp and kitsch. What is being alluded to here is the difference that exists between the mainstream mass culture/corporate use of Bollywood as style to sell goods, versus the use of the same aesthetic features by queer *desis* in the diaspora to read themselves back into Bollywood. Thus, I am drawing attention to the difference between camp as commodity and camp as a mode to cultural and political identity.[4] In order to develop and differentiate between this comparison it is important to begin to think about the recent visibility of Bollywood as a cosmopolitan style that is linked to the queer use of Bollywood by its urban South Asian and diasporic audiences; and the queer use of Bollywood that facilitates it as the new site of the hip and the cool which then gets appropriated by the mainstream cultural and entertainment industries, albeit in simple ways. This chapter, then, is a call for the need to think about supplementing the apolitical uses of Bollywood style by exploring some of its hitherto un-remarked political uses, and as its political uses are made sense of and recreated by queer *desis*. This is a point of departure, a line of flight that takes us away from simple understandings of Bollywood cinema and its popular culture towards considering how queer *desis* appropriate Bollywood, and how this can be understood as different to white mainstream queering strategies that also draw on and recreate popular cultural references from Hollywood cinema, albeit in nuanced ways (as will be explored later in the chapter).

And, it is really this idea of some of Bollywood's promiscuous features around the queer and camp pleasures of gender and sexuality that I want to explore in this chapter, particularly in the diasporic British Asian context as a site in the transnational circulation of Bollywood cinema and popular culture where transformations in meaning are contested and proclaimed. The aesthetics of Bollywood films, not least their songs and dances that are inscribed with culturally-specific mores as well as slippages around gender and sexuality, warrant a consideration of them as promiscuous—moving in and out and in-between heteronormative and queer desires and sensibilities. As a way of moving towards that I will consider how it is now possible to theoretically begin to conceptualise Bollywood in more complex and useful ways. Of late, a number of serious academic studies are giving the popular Hindi cinema of India its due attention (see, for example, Appadurai 1996; Chakravarty 1996; Dwyer 2000; Kaur and Sinha 2005; Kazmi 1999; Mishra 2002; Nandy 1998; Prasad 1998; Rajadhyaksha 1998; Vasudevan 2000; Virdi 2003). Whilst these authors deal with Bollywood cinema and its possible translations in India and/or in the South Asian diasporas, they do not deal explicitly, if at all, with issues of gender and sexuality as also articulated in interpretations of popular Hindi cinema. I aim to suggest, therefore, how it might be possible to dialogue this recent scholarship with queer readings of Bollywood.

I want to use three authors here as starting points for my argument. The first is Ashis Nandy (1998) and the other is Madhava Prasad (1998). Both are based in India and have written about the popular Hindi cinema experience in the Indian subcontinent. I then want to move on to the work of Arjun Appadurai (1996) as a way to think about the translation of the Bollywood cinematic and popular cultural experience as amalgamated into the lives of its British Asian audiences, or for at least those audiences that partake in Bollywood-related activities. Using this threefold theoretical excursion into Bollywood I will then offer a reading of the pleasures of gender and sexuality at a British Asian gay and lesbian club night as a way of arguing for the need to think more about the Bollywood experience in the South Asian diasporas. The chapter also engages with, and brings into dialogue, the three aforementioned studies with the small and important body of work that has appeared in recent years attempting to address queer readings of Bollywood cinema (Gopinath 2000; Kavi 2000; Rao 2000; Waugh 2001), and delineates this research in terms of my own project.

BOLLYWOOD'S SECRET POLITICS OF THE EVERYMAN/WOMAN

Let us begin with Ashis Nandy (1998). Nandy argues that popular Hindi cinema in India gives emphasis to the everyman/woman perspective by stressing the concerns of the people of the slums and the lower middle classes, deploying their informal and tacit theories of politics and society. Using the example of cinema, Nandy is primarily concerned about the social tensions and cultural antagonisms that exist between the bourgeoisie and the upper middle classes on the one hand, and those between the lower middle classes and people living in the slums on the other. For Nandy, and rightly so, popular Hindi cinema comprises the ability to shock the bourgeoisie with the directness, vigour and crudeness of its language and representation, whilst also including them at the same time. As he goes on to say:

> An average, 'normal', Bombay film has to be, to the extent possible, everything to everyone. It has to cut across the myriad ethnicities and lifestyles of India and even of the world that impinges on India. The popular film is low-brow, modernizing India in all its complexity, sophistry, naivete and vulgarity. Studying popular film is studying Indian modernity at its rawest, its crudities laid bare by the fate of traditions in contemporary life and arts. Above all, it is studying caricatures of ourselves (Nandy 1998: 7).

Nandy's idea about a caricature of selfhood can be usefully extended to think about a notion of self-identity, and in this case self-identity as formed through the consumption of Bollywood films, as implicated in a modernity of nation-building in India. This includes ideas about looking to the future, i.e., the promise of post-Independence India, and the disappointment when that promise is constantly broken, for example, in communal riots, bride burning, corruption in public life and so forth. In short, Nandy invites us to think about how popular cinema not merely shapes and is shaped by politics, he invites us to think more about how it also *constitutes the language for a new form of politics* (emphasis is mine), one that includes historical and contemporary analysis and elements of futurism. It is useful to develop and extend Nandy's idea of how we might start thinking about Bollywood as a resource for cultural politics in the South Asian diasporic context—to begin to think about the ways in which Bollywood cinema provides queer *desis* with semantic and visual cues through which they can engage in a cultural politics. But before we get to that via Appadurai, it is also important to heed the words of Madhava Prasad.

IDEOLOGY AND BOLLYWOOD CINEMA

Prasad draws on Marxist ideas of ideology and applies them to popular Hindi cinema (Prasad 1998). He focuses on the period of the seventies in India where he demonstrates that a change in social and political ideology was underway as part of the fragmentation of the post-Independence national consensus which was brought about by shifts in political alignments. For Prasad, these shifts challenged the aesthetic conventions and modes of production of the Indian film industry of the time causing it to split into three categories: art cinema, middle-brow cinema and commercial cinema (ibid.: 118). In terms of the latter category, i.e., commercial cinema or Bollywood, Prasad laments the status quo affirming politics and ideology of this cinema as elaborated through practices of narrative codes and signification. Prasad's focus on Hindi cinema, then, is far from a simple celebration of Bollywood. It is more of a critique of its complicity in the social order of Indian life.

Now Prasad's view is fine up to a certain point as all popular texts have elements of the existing hegemonic social and cultural order mediated within their construction, but the best ones are often those that also challenge prevalent structures and suggest how things might be differently. This is something that Prasad lacks in his analysis of popular Hindi cinema. It is useful to hold on to Prasad's idea of the workings of Bollywood cinema as an ideology, not least extending to think about Bollywood as espousing a predominantly heteronormative ideology. But perhaps it is a more useful formulation of ideology if we are able to think about how ideology exists and how it is able to be reworked and contested in and through the signs and codes which Bollywood cinema might offer us as constituting the language for a new form of politics (Nandy 1998), especially one based around the queer pleasures of gender and sexuality. Furthermore, Prasad's critique of Bollywood cinema's role in hegemonic social formation also operates within the realms of the nation state of India and seldom moves beyond this frame of reference. The appearance of Bollywood songs and dances in the queer spaces of the diaspora requires a careful consideration of the homeland and its diaspora.[5]

BOLLYWOOD AND DIASPORIC MEDIASCAPES

Which leads us on to the work of Arjun Appadurai (1990, 1996). Whilst Nandy and Prasad write about the Indian context, we need to think more about how their useful ideas can be incorporated and translated in the Indian and South Asian diasporic context. This is where the cultural anthropology of Appadurai is instructive. Appadurai offers a useful perspective for understanding the relationship between cultural texts and social experience as elaborated through the concept of the imagination. To rephrase a point that I have just made, popular cultural texts (like Bollywood films) are such because they are embedded in the social worlds of their audiences, sometimes affirming the consensus of that social world and sometimes offering possibilities that suggest new worlds with different ways of being. Appadurai usefully argues that new possibilities are often suggested imaginatively through the production of, and in and through the performance of, sounds and images in texts.

Appadurai is interested in how global social flows are part of a 'disjunctive' order of economies and cultural signs which are played out between 'ethnoscapes—the landscapes of living persons', and 'mediascapes—image-centred, narrative based accounts of strips of reality' (Appadurai 1990: 298).

The availability of mediascapes for diasporic ethnic groups in their countries of settlement is especially pertinent here. Diasporic groups have undergone the experience of deterritorialisation from their places of origin and ethnic mediascapes such as Bollywood offer an audio-visual space for ideas of the homeland and its translations to be negotiated around the world in places of diasporic settlement (cf. Bhabha 1990).

It is the availability of the sounds and images for diasporic ethnic groups in centres of the developed world that help create a diasporic imaginary. This imaginary offers possibilities for comprehending the position of the diasporic subject in the country of settlement and the country of origin as informing each other to produce new sensibilities of being and belonging. Such sensibilities shift between local places of residence and global ideas and cultural flows. The diasporic imaginary becomes part of the everyday of diasporic subjects, as the sounds and images of mediascapes are integrated into the routines and rituals of daily life, as well as the struggles for settlement and belonging.

Appadurai's work, then, opens up the idea of the imagination and its offshoots of fantasy and desire as everyday social practices. The imagination as expressed through dream sequences, songs, music, television, film and stories offers a repertoire of possibilities to grasp the subjects' social world as it articulates with global ideas and cultural processes. This articulation allows for an engagement with the subjects' immediate sense of self, and for the contemplation of a wider set of possible lives. It is the articulation of the local and the global most notably in the cultural negotiations that are taking place between diasporic ideas about the countries of origin and ideas in the countries of settlement that I would like to draw attention to in this chapter. In particular, I would like to focus on the imagination, as it unfolds fantasies and desires of making spaces anew for the diasporic subject especially around the pleasures of queer gender and sexuality in and through the use of Bollywood cinema.

Nandy's cultural politics about nation-building, Prasad's warnings of the workings of ideology and Appadurai's claims about the diasporic imagination can be usefully amalgamated together as a theoretical excursion in order to make sense of some of the translations of Bollywood cinema that are taking place in the diasporic urban ethnoscape of the British Asian gay and lesbian club night. Before moving on to an analysis of this site, let us consider some queer readings of Bollywood cinema that have been put forward of late and that are taken up for further elaboration in this chapter as dialoguing with these three aforementioned cultural critics.

QUEERYING BOLLYWOOD

A special issue of the *Journal of Homosexuality* (Grossman 2000) first brought together a number of essays on queer Asian cinema. Whilst it was noted in this collection that East Asian cinemas, in particular films from Hong Kong and China, have been able to deal more overtly in both aesthetic and in content with queer themes and representations, popular Indian cinema was still operating at the level of implicit queer suggestions in its aesthetics and content, or that it was the queer audiences' rereading of the heteronormative film text that allowed for queer sensibilities to be detected and analysed. The essay by Gopinath (2000) is illuminating in this respect.

Gopinath draws on cultural theory and feminist audience studies to argue that Bollywood cinema provides queer diasporic audiences with the means by which to re-imagine and re-territorialise the homeland by making it the locus of queer desire and pleasure. Gopinath is interested in tracing the possibilities of 'interpretive interventions and appropriations' made by queer diasporic audiences of Bollywood films (Gopinath 2000: 284). She employs a 'queer diasporic viewing practice' in order to see articulations of same-sex desire in particular examples of popular Hindi cinema throughout the diegesis of the film, even when the film has an orthodox heterosexual ending. Rather than attempt to look for gays and lesbians in Bollywood, she is more interested in 'looking for the moments emerging at the fissures of rigidly heterosexual structures that can be transformed into queer imaginings' (ibid.). Gopinath goes on to read the possibilities offered by images that suggest gay, lesbian and hijra or transgendered modes of being.

As a result of attempting such tracings, the queer diasporic subjectivity that is put forward by Gopinath is one that is created at the intersection of dominant Euro-American constructions of gay and lesbian identity that are brought into dialogue and negotiations between the spaces of multiple homes, communities and nations across the cultural registers of East and West (ibid.). This is a useful formulation of the queer diasporic subjectivity as it does not privilege a European mode of understanding or performing of queer cultural identity at the cost of its Asian counterpart, but rather asks for an analysis of the communicative dialogue that is possible when the two different sensibilities interact. Whilst Gopinath posits this fascinating exchange between European and Asian queer cultural identity at a theoretical level she never really demonstrates the articulation of the two together. There is an implied tendency within the work of Gopinath to privilege the queer diaspora and readings taking place within it (i.e., as simply reformulating or re-imagining the homeland) without due consideration to the queer possibilities in the homeland, or the reciprocating social flows between the homeland and its diasporas. This is a facet of queer cultural and social phenomena that begs further discussion and analysis at the urban ethnoscape of the South Asian gay and lesbian club night and hence is offered as an addition to the work of Gopinath (as explored later in the chapter). The disjunctive flows (Appadurai 1990) occurring between the homeland and the diaspora, and vice versa, are suggested in this chapter through a focus on the translations of Bollywood song and dance sequences in the queer club nights of the diaspora, and also of Bollywood cinema's increasing attention to queer themes and representations of late.

The essays by Rao (2000) and Kavi (2000) provide us with an understanding of some of the key motifs and signifying codes that feature throughout Bollywood films and how these are interpreted by its queer audiences against the grain of its ostensibly heterosexual intentions. For example, Rao describes the motifs of *yaar* (friend and/ or lover) and *yaari* (friendship) as expressed in the lyrics and picturisation of song sequences as recapitulated in queer subculture as a yearning for an affectionate same-sex relationship (Rao 2000: 304–5). Kavi outlines the changing image of the male hero in Hindi films over some five decades to suggest how the contemporary male body, and in particular the semi-clad and gym-fit physique of nineties' star Salman Khan, has been ambiguously paraded and eroticised on screen and whose appeal goes beyond straight pleasures and desires (Kavi 2000: 308–10). Furthermore, Rao reveals the social practices of urban Indian cinema going that are also made queer in the dark spaces of the cinema hall patronised largely by men. Here, close physical contact and same-sex intimacy can and does occur, and as Rao describes one of his visits to the cinema, '[a]s the lights went off, the action began, so to speak, both on the screen and off it' (Rao 2000: 304). Both Rao and Kavi's work, then, suggest that the formulation of Indian queer identity, and gay urban Indian identity in particular, as taking shape in relation to the hierarchy of male sexuality (where men have greater access and control to public spaces over women in which to express their same-sex desires and displays, albeit implicitly) and where subversion and rereading against the grain of the heteronormative Bollywood diegesis is often a recurring strategy of existence. Extending this work, then, does the homosocial polysemy of popular film music also permit queer identifications in Bollywood's transnational circuits?

An essay by Thomas Waugh (2001), although published elsewhere, can also be considered alongside the aforementioned authors on queer Bollywood. Developing ideas of audience rereadings of same-sex sexual display and subversion in Hindi films, and by drawing on the anthropology of Lawrence Cohen's exploration of male same-sex activities in Varanasi (formerly known as Benares), India (Cohen 1995a, 1995b), Waugh examines 'the profuse and rigidly ambiguous indigenous male–male sexual iconographies' in contemporary Bollywood cinema (Waugh 2001: 282). By exploring queer readings of male-buddy moments in films such as *Sholay* (Flames, dir. Ramesh Sippy, 1975) and *Main Khiladi Tu Anari* (I'm the Player You're the Amateur, dir. Sameer Malkan, 1994), Waugh outlines how the cultural devices of *khel* (play/playfulness) and *dosti* (friendship) between the on-screen heroes (which involves the use of sexual innuendos, phallic symbols and the close proximity of male bodies in intimate postures) can be understood as illustrating an implicit homosocial sphere that operates within and yet beyond the predominant heterosexual reel and real life (ibid.: 292). Waugh usefully posits the devices of same-sex *khel* and *dosti* as challenging and redefining the rules of heterosexual gazes and desires as the dominant and only modes of seeing and interacting (ibid.: 293) that allow queer audiences to view themselves and their heroes and heroines as visible, invisible, polyvocal and ambiguous (ibid.: 296). Elaborating Waugh further: how does the transnational circulation of Hindi film music invest these textual ambiguities with new possibilities?

Let us now incorporate these queer readings of popular Hindi cinema within the theoretical framework of Nandy, Prasad and Appadurai as formulated so far. Gopinath, Rao, Kavi and Waugh demonstrate specifically the sentiments of Nandy's hypotheses of popular Indian cinema as consisting of tacit or secret cultural politics relating to the projects of self-identity and nationhood. Such politics become further pressing and engaging as these queer readings insist that the queer in Bollywood needs to be included as part of the discussion of Bollywood cinema and its audiences, both locally and globally. Developing the work of Prasad, how might we account for the reworking of the heterosexual ideology of gender and sexuality in queer Bollywood spaces? Using the insights of Appadurai, and in order to begin to understand the diasporic queer urban ethnoscape of the gay and lesbian club, to what extent are the social strategies and cultural devices as described by Gopinath, Rao, Kavi and Waugh also prevalent or translated at this site? Furthermore, is the homeland simply reconfigured in the queer diaspora (cf. Gopinath 2000), or does the homeland also respond to the queer diaspora, or vice versa, albeit in secret ways?

THE DIASPORIC URBAN ETHNOSCAPE OF THE SOUTH ASIAN GAY AND LESBIAN CLUB NIGHT

The qualitative and participant observations that I draw on and outline in this section were witnessed and experienced at a particular Asian gay and lesbian club in the UK. But the description that follows could be in any one of the growing Asian gay and lesbian club nights in Birmingham, Leicester, London, or Manchester (all UK-based)[6], or even perhaps in New York[7] and elsewhere around the world where similar queer Bollywood activities are taking place. To think of such a club night as a diasporic urban ethnoscape (cf. Appadurai 1990) one is drawing attention to the social and cultural interactions that manifest themselves between people and their mediascapes as drawing on signs and codes from various homelands that have travelled, metaphorically and literally, arriving at a new place of settlement and offering multiple or at least new modes of being that shift between the homeland and the place of residence. The description of the club night is offered here as a sketch or template from which to extrapolate and engage with some of the theoretical issues and queer textual readings that have been put forward earlier in the chapter.

Figure 5.1: 'Live life for who u r...' An advertising banner from the Manchester (UK) based Club Zindagi's website that draws on Bollywood aesthetics and advocates a message for social and sexual liberation

To describe the club night as a 'gay and lesbian' one, is in keeping with how those queer *desis* who regularly party-on at the club also choose to describe it as such. The term 'gay and lesbian', then, is used as a short hand for the club's eclectic clientele along sexual lines, but this is in no way to exclude its other diverse people, sexualities and personalities that also frequent the clubs. So here one is also thinking about Asian drag queens, hijras or transgendered people, cross-dressers, bisexuals, queer-friendly straights, straight couples, and those who might just be exploring or passing through.

The kinds of people who regularly attend this club in terms of their ethnic backgrounds include Asians (predominantly South Asians and also other Asians), Africans and Caribbeans, and Caucasians too—a metropolitan and racially diverse mixture of people. The diversity of participants here is indicative of the cultural and social exchanges and possibilities at this diasporic site of reception, a cosmopolitan nodal point on the global movement of Bollywood music. Thus, an understanding of queer *desi* identities in this club space needs to be located and explored through the different social registers and cultural performances of race and ethnicity, gender and sexuality as articulating together.

The particular club venue under analysis has a large dance floor that is square in shape, somewhat similar to that of a high school hall. At the front of the dance hall is a raised stage. On the back wall of the stage there is a white canvas—similar to that of a small cinema screen; in fact it is the very screen upon which images from Bollywood movies are projected. Opposite the stage and on the other side of the dance floor is the DJ booth encased in a room with a large window that oversees the dance floor space. In the centre of the dance hall ceiling is a large shiny disco ball that hangs as the centrepiece amidst the other sophisticated discotheque lighting. The club night is almost always on a Friday night, so there is a start of the weekend euphoria that is articulated with the prowess of gender and sexual pleasures. These pleasures include 'girls eyeing girls eyeing boys eyeing boys eyeing girls' and more, and almost everyone is overcome with a fever to dance and exalt their bodily performances on the dance floor. One of the friends I was there with on one night suggested to me that it was 'like being at an Indian wedding party after all the official ritual and ceremonies have taken place, only this is a bit more fun, more risky'—an affirmation of the secret politics (cf. Nandy 1998) taking place at this venue if ever I had heard it. In fact there seems to be a continuity, here, as well as a new line of flight being suggested between the diaspora's appropriation of the homeland through Bollywood, and the queer diaspora's uses of the same. Bollywood movie clips and songs and dances are often used at South Asian weddings and other community gatherings such as beauty pageants throughout the diaspora. The articulation of social desires and fantasies relating to the homeland are also possibly similar—an articulation of referents from the homeland and the place of settlement professing dual or multiple cultural sensibilities. However, the issue of sexuality is often an unspoken and silent register in the enactment of cultural identities at the diasporic community events and this is where the queer *desi* club night offers an explicit engagement with issues of gender and sexuality. The space of the club is highlighted further as a marker of gender and sexual difference within the South Asian diaspora itself.

Gladrags are flaunted and they help the boys to look sharp and the girls sharper still. Vibrant colours and South Asian dress styles coalesce with the best of Western haute couture. The music is often a 70 per cent mixture of Bollywood, bhangra, Arabic pop, rai and Anglo-Asian fusion music, and the remainder a blend of RnB, ragga and hip hop, with the odd dash of pop thrown in for good measure; the tracks of Kylie Minogue often feature as pop classics in this club. These musical genres are significant not only in terms of their heralding of the club's audiences' eclectic cultural identities, but also important in terms of how these genres signify certain kinds of identities that are enabled on the dance floor through a performance of the self. These can be fluid gender and sexual identities that are engaging with some of the more promiscuous melodies and lyrics of the songs from each of the genres, and at the same time urban and racialised identities being contemplated through a singing and dancing out of some of the more urban politicised lyrics and music— British bhangra, Anglo-Asian fusion, rap, ragga and hip hop being cases in point here (on the fusion and social possibilities of these music genres see Sharma et al. 1996 and Dudrah 2002b). Not only, then, are South Asian gay and lesbian identities constructed and celebrated in the queer *desi* club space, they are also articulated with issues of brown skin and ethnic identities that negotiate against the inequalities of racism, gender and sexuality that exist not only in heteronormative spaces but also in predominantly white gay and lesbian spaces too.[8] The queer *desi* club is also a safe space and its dance floor is an interesting outlet that allows these kinds of performances to take place. It signals a space for identities on the dance floor to be made mobile through a play of actual bodily movements and embodied gestures that use fantasy and the imagination to interact with the music to create a queer ambience in the club.

Amidst the performance of selves on the dance floor, one can also witness some of Bollywood's key motifs of *yaar* and *yaari* (Rao 2000), the signifying codes of the eroticised body (Kavi 2000) and the cultural devices of *khel* and *dosti* (Waugh 2001) as acted out and translated in this diasporic space. In order to illustrate this performance, I want to draw on three examples that I experienced and partook in at the club on more than one occasion. In the first example, I wish to recount the numerous Bollywood tracks that are often played, both in their original and remixed versions, that feature lyrics professing love for one's *yaar* or the desire to be in *yaari*. Thus, for instance, '*Mera yaar bura dildaara...*' (My friend/lover is truly a braveheart), '*Tu mera yaar, tu mera pyaar...*' (You are my friend/lover, you are my love), '*Aaja ve mere yaar...*' (Come on my friend/lover). Here, the notion of *yaar* and *yaari* is clearly reread and subverted from its heterosexual intentions and recast as a queer sensibility and display of same-sex affection. Moreover, this rereading of *yaar/yaari* is further complexified as it is translated amidst the fusion of different musical genres (Bollywood and bhangra beats and Afro-American rapping) and made sense of in this diaspora and cosmopolitan club space. Not only is the original heterosexual version of *yaar/yaari* changed into a queer one, the queer *yaar/yaari* is further nuanced according to its construction that takes place in the mixture of international music genres that signify new musical sounds and fluid social identities in the UK. Here, queer identities both coalesce with and negotiate ethnic and racial identities too. In this way, the homosocial polysemy of popular Hindi film music permits queer identifications that are reworked and nuanced with added meaning and relevance for lives of queer *desis* across Bollywood's transnational circuits.

In the second example I wish to recall the movement of bodies whilst dancing and their relationship to the Bollywood images played on the white canvas on stage. On this occasion, the dance floor is packed and we are halfway through the club night. Sweating bodies are infused with cologne and decorated with colourful glitters that groove the night away. One track comes to an end and the other begins. The new track is 'Chaiyya, chaiyya' (Walk in the Shadow of Love) from the film *Dil Se...* (From the Heart, dir. Mani Ratnam, 1998). The crowd shouts in excitement and begins to mimic the dance steps of actor Shahrukh Khan and his gypsy-girl consort (Malaika

Arora-Khan) from the film, with hips swaying, pelves thrusting and arms waving about in the air[9] (see Figure 5.2).

Figure 5.2: Dancing on a moving train: Dance moves from the 'Chaiyya, chaiyya' track from the film *Dil Se...* that are recreated in the queer club space

A momentary lapse occurs between the on-screen mediascape in the club and the song playing over the club's sound system. The audio of the song is a few seconds ahead of its projected image. The 'Chaiyya, chaiyya' clip on-screen has also been edited and is interspersed with songs from other Bollywood movies; of note is the flashing torso of Salman Khan while he gyrates. The dancing bodies on the dance floor as a few paces ahead of the dancing figures in the moving image during this moment is telling of the ways in which gender and sexual pleasures are aestheticised in different yet related ways. In the film Shahrukh Khan is mesmerised after having just met his on-screen heroine, Manisha Koirala, and breaks into song and dance affirming his new found heterosexual love. In the club the crowd also register this filmic moment and yet simultaneously reclaim and acknowledge the song as one of their queer anthems. The straight aesthetics on the screen are there to be seen as part of the literal backdrop to the club's setting and also to be mimicked and performed in queer ways—the singing and dancing on the dance floor is a few paces ahead of its on-screen version both literally and symbolically. The further editing of the *Dil Se...* film clip with images of the naked torso of Salman Khan also deliberately queers and displaces the dominant straight aesthetics of the clip to enable new pleasures around gender, sexuality and the dancing of the body. The physical use of the body in dance, here, plays with conventional and expected patterns of heteronormativity. Signifiers of perceived masculine and feminine traits are used by both genders, mingled with Bollywood, Westernised and black urban street moves and queer displays of eclectic sexual identities, thereby creating a stylised camp performance. Within this performativity a caricature of conservative heterosexual expectations of how men and women should conduct themselves as representing their sexualities is also set into play. Males on males, females on females, and male and females alternate with each other playing up 'butch' and 'passive' body movements and dance gestures and thereby hyperbole normative gender and sexual ideologies. Through feminine and masculine screams, yells, and screeches and through the repertoire of their dress and vivid colours— almost costume-like—the club revellers also exaggerate and play up their own camp performances. Caricature, in this instance, works to recreate a performance about heterosexuality and its limits in order to make way for their queer semantics and also to render specific performativities about South Asian queerness in this club space.

The third instance exemplifies how *khel* takes place in the club and consolidates an understanding of *dosti* that is communicative in a social cementing sense and also in terms of its queer sexual connotations. The track 'Koyi kahen' (People will Say) from the film *Dil Chahta Hai* (What the Heart Wants, dir. Farhan Akhtar, 2001) is played which draws the dancing crowd together singing almost in unison and jumping up and down in ways that are similar to how the lead actors and actresses dance in the filmed version (see Figure 5.3).[10]

Boys turn to dance with boys and girls with girls as well as the exchange of other gender and sexuality combinations. The *dosti* that is forged in this *khel* is commensurate with the lyrics of the song. In the movie the singers proclaim their disavowal of rigid societal norms and elder and peer generational pressures in order to forge a new way for themselves. In the space of the queer South Asian club the translations here are quite straightforward to decipher. *Dosti* (friendship) are made in the *khel* (play) about being different to straight

Figure 5.3: (From Left to right) Saif Ali Khan, Aamir Khan and Akshaye Khanna dance to 'Koyi kahen' from the film *Dil Chahta Hai* that is used and translated to perform queer *dostis* (friendships) at the club night

societal norms and expectations. A cultural solidarity is exhibited in and through the *dostis* that profess gender and sexual difference on the dance floor and partake in a promiscuous *khel* wherein several bodies are up close and personal—touching, sweating and being sexually suggestive. Yet, the *khel* is promiscuous only up to a point. Like many other devices of playfulness in South Asian cultural traditions the *khel* here also works through suggestion and within its own boundary limits. Whilst there is full-on same-sex kissing and touching it very rarely becomes x-rated. The suggestion of same-sex sexual display and affection is far more titillating and provocative than going beyond it (i.e., flirtations of sexual innuendos and the close proximity of bodies in intimate postures and gestures). Also interesting here is that there is no dark room in the club, and this appears to be the case also for the other UK *desi* gay and lesbian clubs that I attended.[11] Whereas the heterosexual ideology of Bollywood is done away with in the *khel* of the club, the signs and codes of how heterosexuality is coded and performed in Bollywood, as imposing an order of gender and sexual conduct, is reconfigured by Bollywood's queer patrons.[12] In mainstream Bollywood one rarely sees explicit sexual exhibitionism as it is often laced with coyness, innuendos and metaphors of suggestion. This is also the case in the South Asian gay and lesbian club. It appears that the same songs and dances in Bollywood films that are used to signify sexual effects as a way of getting around Indian censorship rules are also used in a similar way to avert the censure of heteronormativity, through bodily decorum, playfulness and same-sex suggestion performed on the dance floor. And herein lies another difference between the diasporic South Asian gay and lesbian scene and its white Western counterpart. Public displays of sexual mores that are an exploration and illustration of selfhood are deliberately coded through Bollywood mores as providing a social etiquette through which to conduct oneself in the club space. This public etiquette stresses cultural difference in relation to other queer scenes at the point of sexually avant garde and liberating performances that operate within cultural codes of excess and celebration (i.e., of Bollywood), and certainly not x-rated overspill.

Just as there are differences and cultural specificities, there are also similarities to be drawn here between white gay and lesbian club culture and its use of mainstream pop songs and Hollywood film stars to express different genders and sexualities. For example, feminist readings of Hollywood have drawn our attention to a number of extra-cinematic identificatory practices (cf. Stacey 1993). These include posturing, mimicry, dressing-up, irony, exaggeration, performing oneself like a film star, deploying the stars' masculine/feminine qualities, using the star's sexual appeal, and relishing in how the star has excelled at surviving the social order of the day in the reel/diegetic world on the screen, and perhaps even in real/actual life. Equally, Bollywood has no limit to the number of its stars that have achieved demi-God status in South Asia and its diasporic societies over the years, both male and female, and who have been appropriated by different sections of Bollywood's audiences, not least its gay and lesbian audiences.[13]

In addition to these star qualities and the appropriation of Bollywood idols, one is also arguing that central to the performance of gender and sexualities in the South Asian gay and lesbian club is a notion of pleasure that is important for sections of Bollywood's queer diasporic audiences. In particular, I am drawing on the notion of pleasure as it has been widely used in the discipline of cultural studies where it has focused on the pleasures of the text (for example, Regan 1992). Here, pleasures of the text have been described through the ability of the audiences' cultural capital to read, partake and identify with particular forms of popular culture. It is an idea of the audiences' familiarity with the text's codes and conventions that contribute to an aesthetic, emotional and, as in the case of dance as cited earlier, a physical enjoyment of the form. In the queer South Asian club space the pleasures of the Bollywood film text are also extended and translated in terms of queer desires and sensibilities of *yaar/yaari*, *dosti*, and *khel*, and the performativity of the eroticised body.

IS THE QUEER REREAD IN BOLLYWOOD, OR IS BOLLYWOOD INHERENTLY QUEER?

Let us finally consider whether the homeland is simply reconfigured in the queer diaspora (cf. Gopinath 2000), or whether the homeland also responds to the queer diaspora, or vice versa, albeit in secret ways? What has been proposed in this chapter is that a simple reading of Bollywood's use in the diaspora as being subverted and reread should be resisted. Evidently, as has been illustrated in the earlier discussion, there are aspects of subversion and translation of Bollywood's heteronormative boy-meets-girl romances that are taking place in the queer diaspora. Yet, this is nothing unique as queer cultures, almost everywhere, often appropriate straight social texts and discourses for their own means and thereby create a new language through which to communicate and express themselves. The 'newness' in the queer South Asian diaspora is its constituting of a tacit and secret politics that is in dialogue with its Bollywood sources as informing and producing each other anew. The secret politics are also becoming more visible and encoded into the workings of mainstream Bollywood that suggest a reconfiguring of the relationship between the homeland and the diaspora in a more problematic and complex way. In order to elaborate on this I want to suggest two lines of inquiry for further research and analysis.

First, the aesthetic and traditional conventions of Bollywood need to be considered further as hybrid, 'queer' and 'camp' from their outset.[14] In particular I am thinking of how the early development of popular Indian cinema has always been eclectic, even if it has not been acknowledged as such. Early twentieth-century films (for example, *Raja Harischandra*, dir. Dada Sahib Phalke, 1913) had either men playing female roles or prostitutes who were hired as actresses; acting in Indian cinema at that time was considered a social taboo for 'respectable' women. Such films were paradoxically used to create and confirm a social order of heterosexuality and patriarchy, but how might one also account for the early queer desires and secret politics that were enabled by such transgressions on screen that were composed in the articulation of the 'camp' and 'non-camp', the 'queer' and the 'straight'? If such a line of thought can be developed further out of historical and contemporary inquiry, is it possible to argue that South Asian queer spaces, both in the diaspora and in the homeland, not only signify from and reread or appropriate Bollywood, but that such queer signs are and have been pre-existing in the formation of Bollywood from its outset? Examples for further testing and elaboration could include the 'camp' theatrical performances of early Hindu mythologicals where men dressed up to play women characters, and early heroines who played masculine and 'butch' action roles.[15] The Parsi and regional theatres which included stories situated in the *kotha* (courtesan houses and brothels) with their co-existing narratives of heterosexuality and lesbianism is another possible instance.[16] By bringing the ideas of Nandy (1998) into conversation with the queer readings put forward here, then, it is possible to argue that in a caricature of selfhood queer Bollywood is not only a matter of the 'queer readings' that 'queer audiences' bring to the text (as put forward by Gopinath) but rather Bollywood's investment in caricature makes it a rich cultural resource where meanings of 'queer' and 'camp' can be readily created and contested. Thus, even the manifest heteronormative content is queered by representational excess that marginalises questions of authenticity (of straightness for example), since both queer and straight are equally caricatured; they are representations of an ordered and constructed world (i.e., of heteronormativity) and its slippages, that makes spaces for insights into new worlds (of queer possibilities).

The second line of thought acknowledges the shift and changes that are taking place in more recent Bollywood films in which queer themes and representations are becoming slightly more visible and perhaps more fluid. Therefore, is Bollywood listening to and in dialogue with queer South Asian cultural politics both in the homeland

and in the diaspora, although at an early embryonic stage? Three brief examples will suffice here. First, the gay urban Indian kiss in *Rules: Pyar Ka Super Hit Formula* (Rules: Love's Winning Formula, dir. Parvati Balagopalan, 2003) which is not demonised or estranged through its on-screen aesthetics. Second, the queer *khel* between Shahrukh Khan (who plays Aman) and Saif Ali Khan (Rohit) in *Kal Ho Naa Ho* (Tomorrow May Not Be, dir. Nikhil Advani, 2003), set in the diasporic city of New York, that is wrongly interpreted by Saif Ali Khan's housemaid as the two characters are in a gay relationship. The film sets up a heterosexual love triangle between Aman, Rohit and Naina Catherine Kapur Patel (Preity Zinta). However, sexual innuendos between the two male characters and scenes of their bodies in close intimate proximity to each other are rife in this film (see Figure 5.4). The two characters also flirt with camp performativity and dance together with added suggestions of homosexuality, albeit through the use of humour as a backdrop. Even the film's climax is open to a promiscuous queer reading. As Aman lies dying on a hospital bed, the two male characters reach a compromise over their individual love for Naina, whilst holding and embracing each other

Figure 5.4: Shahrukh Khan (left) and Saif Ali Khan in queer *khel* in the film *Kal Ho Naa Ho*

closely. During this scene, Naina is seen outside of the frame of the two characters, outside of the hospital room in which Aman and Rohit make their personal agreement with each other.

Finally, the conversation that takes place between Aman (Rahul Bose) and Chameli (Kareena Kapoor) in the film *Chameli* (Scented/ Healing Flower, dir. Sudhir Mishra, 2004), while they are sheltering from the heavy rain under the same archway in Mumbai and begin to get to know each other. When Aman realises that one of Chameli's friends, Raja, is gay and is in love with a male cross-dresser, Hasina, he initially appears surprised. During their conversation, Chameli asks Aman whether he feels that there is something wrong with two men in a relationship together. Aman hesitantly responds 'no' and qualifies his response saying he has male friends who are gay. Chameli goes on to declare that there is nothing 'abnormal' about gay relationships as long as there is love in them—'*bus pyar hona chayen*'. Reasons for such noticeable queer representations in contemporary Bollywood cinema owe much to the rise of queer politics in India and the courting of diaspora as an audience for Bollywood.[17] However, what needs to be investigated further is whether or not there are genuine queer possibilities opening up here, or if they are simply being subsumed within the dominant heteronormative workings of Bollywood cinema?

As a way of conclusion to this chapter let us return to the opening remarks made about the Selfridge's celebration of Bollywood popular culture that has been juxtaposed with the diasporic ethnoscape of the queer South Asian club. The example of Bollywood film and music culture's translation at the gay and lesbian club are telling of the secret politics that the Selfridges store could only take on board in very subtle ways. The Selfridge's camp and kitsch that was lifted from Bollywood was not quite right. It was not sure of how to fully deal with these aspects other than through mere suggestion, and it focused more on making a profit by trying to cater to the highest spending pound and thereby making the consumption of Bollywood safe and yet exotic. What needs to be observed and commented on is precisely how queer culture is increasingly being appropriated to market and promote consumption. Thus, what happens to camp when it turns into commodity? One is not arguing that the South Asian gay and lesbian clubs are the only place for different and potentially progressive Bollywood-influenced genders and sexualities to flourish, but that they are a space in which the diasporic imaginary can shift more usefully between the place of residence or the new homeland (i.e., Britain) and the originating homeland (i.e., South Asia), and wherein both the homeland and the diaspora can be brought into dialogue with each other in ways beyond the exotica of orientalism. Furthermore, the use of Bollywood in the gay and lesbian club scene illustrates one of the internal fissures of the wider South Asian diaspora where considerations of gender and sexual difference can often be marginalised or excluded.[18] The direct enactment and performance of gender and sexuality in the queer club space interrogates the nation and its diaspora as in need of reconfiguration through an engagement with such issues. In these ways, the social interactions taking place at the gay and lesbian club also more appropriately draw on, flaunt and recreate the original queer and hybrid composite aesthetic and traditional forms of the popular Hindi cinema in ways that have yet to be understood more thoroughly.

6

BETWEEN AND BEYOND BOLLYWOOD AND HOLLYWOOD

This chapter considers Bollywood cinema in its moments of transition, amidst charges made against it of simply copying Hollywood films and storylines; in terms of the globalisation of its film industry and some of the possibilities that arise from this; and, also in terms of the aesthetic and social developments of the cinema as it is used by diasporic South Asian film-makers in their work. The sociological imagination is put to use to consider the developing landscape of popular Hindi cinema in the era of globalisation in terms of potential outcomes. These are suggested by drawing attention to the cultures of meaning–making that exist between and beyond Bollywood and Hollywood cinemas, how their key players and institutions (i.e., producers, financiers, directors and nation states) might forge relationships in the contemporary moment, and the range of aesthetic and representational options that are made available to audiences through the mixture of two or more cinemas. The chapter ends with a caveat that places these somewhat fluid developments alongside traditional and more deep-seated Orientalist constructions about South Asian representations that are produced anew, also in the present.

COPYING HOLLYWOOD OR CULTURAL MIMICRY?

One of the accusations often labelled at Bollywood cinema is that it is a 'copy', or 'a rip-off' of mainstream Hollywood storylines. Such accusations not only come from conservative Hindi film commentators (for example, Ahmed 1992), some Western academics or reporters (for example, Cook 1996: 861; Malcolm 1989), but even from some sections of Bollywood's audiences too.[1] In the former two categories, when such charges are levelled against Bollywood films, they are less to do with offering an informed critique and more to do with unapprised commentary of the cinema. Bollywood audiences, not only in India but around the world, have been shown more usefully to apply these accusations sparingly as a form of discerning spectatorship and informed critique that is aware of the Hollywood sources being used but that have been recast in 'bad' Bollywood productions where the cast and film crew could have done a better job at adopting those references in the mould of Bollywood cinema (Banaji 2004; Dudrah 2002a: 30–31).

The terms 'copy' or 'rip-off' tend to imply that Bollywood cinema is a plagiarism or cheap imitation of Hollywood and can be part of a criticism that is often loaded with Western signs and meanings of power and difference that are only able to demarcate 'other' cultures and audio-visual systems as inferior. Hollywood blockbuster films are able to lay claim to being the hegemonic centre of mass film appeal the world over due, in part, to their production and global distribution that arise from multi-million dollar budgets. Such budgets are part of the neo-colonial order of things in which maximum monetary profit is the order of the day (Gomery 1998; Moran 1998). Fortunately, audiences do not easily buy into and make a film successful solely on the basis of production values that are enshrined by big budgets. Those eager to dismiss Bollywood need to engage with its mass appeal as one arising out of complex emotions, feelings, values, and imaginative representations which cannot be offered by Hollywood alone, and often at a fraction of the cost. There are in operation incomparable economies of scale in terms of the production of Bollywood movies when compared to Hollywood (see Gokulsing and Dissanayake 1998: 102; Ganti 2004: 53–62 on Bollywood film production), but this does not detract from the pleasure and popularity that Bollywood enjoys with its audiences.

Furthermore, the idea of a 'copy or imitation' of Hollywood is one too easily applied to non-Western cinemas when they may adapt or develop an idea taken from mainstream Hollywood films. Such an approach tends to forget that Hollywood films often appropriate novels or stories that were never intended for the big screen but this is never viewed as a copy. Also, Hollywood film directors are often influenced by film-makers in the developing world but this is rarely appreciated. Quentin Tarrantino's deployment of the action aesthetics of popular Hong Kong cinema would be a case in point.

How might we respond to the charges levelled at Bollywood cinema as simply copying Hollywood in an appropriate and productive way? Perhaps one of the central concerns of the assemblage of popular cinema, from its production through to distribution, is to market its product—the film—which itself is an imitation of life. The assemblage of cinema produces an illusion that is offered first in the dream palace of the cinema and then the smaller dream spaces in the home via video or DVD and then television. Cinema, then, imitates life and various cinemas often borrow from each other. However, rather than cast away Bollywood's imitation of life and the illusions that it fosters as partly rearticulated from Hollywood as blatant bootlegging, Homi Bhabha's (1994) work on cultural mimicry is useful here as a way of dealing with the imitation of Hollywood filmic lives that Bollywood sources through its own idiom and cinematic assemblage.

Bhabha's idea of mimicry is formulated at the intersection of Lacanian psychoanalysis and colonial cultural history wherein colonial authority through its legislature, discourse and governance is shown to have sought to create a mimic of itself; a 'desire for a reformed and recognizable Other, as a subject of a difference that is almost the same, but not quite' (ibid.: 86). Bhabha cites the example of the colonial brown *saahib* in India who was created and employed by his colonial masters to conduct their work by a way of mediation between their colonial subjects in order to maintain control. However, the production of a 'recognisable Other' as a mimic is constructed around ambivalence, through continuous slippage, excess and difference of what it purports to be representing. In this way, Bhabha argues that mimicry is also a sign of a double articulation. On the one hand this articulation works as a 'strategy of reform, regulation and discipline, which appropriates the Other as it visualises power' (ibid.), and this is a menacing strategy. On the other hand this menacing aspect of mimicry 'is its double vision which in disclosing the ambivalence of colonial discourse also disrupts its authority' (Bhabha 1994: 88). The disruption of colonial authority through the excess and slippage of mimicry splinters and unmasks the camouflage of colonial power and enunciates possibilities of becoming that are no longer solely determined by disciplined or controlled forms of power. Mimicry, then, can be extended further to think about how social becoming and subjectivities that arise from the vestiges of power (colonial, disciplined, visual) lead us elsewhere, while using those sources and referents in exaggerated, ironic and parodied ways.

Such elaborate modes of cultural mimicry are often used within Bollywood films to translate Western differences and power hierarchies for Bollywood viewers. Let us consider two examples here as cases in point from the films *Sholay* (Flames, dir. Ramesh Sippy, 1974) and *Main Hoon Na* (I'm Here Now, dir. Farah Khan, 2004).

In the first film, *Sholay*, one of the most well-known Bollywood films of all time, there is the mimic of the English colonial jailor played by comic actor Asrani. During the comic jail scene the film's heroes Veeru (Dharmendra) and Jai (Amitabh Bachchan)—two crooks with hearts of gold—have been caught and sent to prison for one of their many thefts. In fact, they have deliberately staged their capture via an accomplice and go to jail in order to gain the reward placed on them by the state, and then intend to break out and split the reward with their accessory. Veeru and Jai spend their brief time in jail—a matter of weeks if not days—almost at a leisurely pace, biding their time until they make their escape. They meet the jailor and decide to have fun with him at his expense. Asrani is cast as a Hitler-esque leader. He is small in stature, dressed in a militarised brown outfit, baton in hand, and dons a hairstyle and moustache mimicking that of Hitler himself. His body posture is stiff and his manner of speaking is loud and aggressive, yet he is inept at his job as he falls fowl to the pranks of Veeru and Jai (see Figure 6.1). As if to cover up his inabilities as a jailor he repeatedly reminds the inmates that he is 'a jailor of the times of the British' as a threat of potential discipline and punishment. This threat is ignored by the inmates who often look away in bemusement and also by the music that accompanies the jailor's walk—a comedic parody of 'for he's a jolly good fellow' set to a military-style drum roll. The Hitler-esque jailor in *Sholay* provides us with a sign of mimicry in popular Hindi

Figure 6.1: The actor Asrani plays a Hitler-esque jailor in the film *Sholay* through cultural mimicry

cinema that is composed out of the remnants of India's colonial past and its thrust towards a project of independence and modernisation that serves as a critique on state forms of penal control and governance in India of the seventies. Not only is the jailor an exaggerated and ambivalent sign of difference within the prison— he is shown to be overtly fascist and also a relic of the British Raj— but that his accentuated excess around that ambivalence is what undoes the very power that he wishes to profess and hold on to: 'I am a jailor of the times of the British.' This makes way for Veeru and Jai to unmask his camouflage as a competent figure of authority that allows them to ridicule him and to mount their escape from an establishment of the state that is meant to keep them in order. By doing away with the jailor's caricatures of Britishness and colonial authority—they make him burn his hand by picking up a heated metal rod placed sneakily under a basket for him to discover—and making their escape from prison, they seek to be elsewhere and become another possibility outside of the punishing faction of the state apparatus that is performed and exposed through mimicry.

If in Hindi cinema mimicry can reveal the vestiges of colonial authority and control and the simultaneous possibility of its dismantling by social subjects, then it can also illustrate the visual control of that power as it is reconfigured through the lens of Bollywood. Hollywood is seen as the big brother of commercial cinemas the world over—to be aspired to and to be left in awe of, particularly in its big budget spectaculars. Yet this wonder and bedazzlement that it inspires is also recast to fit the nuances and developments in the cultural landscape of popular Hindi cinema's audiences. Let us qualify this point by using the second example from the film *Main Hoon Na*. This film uses and quotes cinematic referents not only from Hollywood but more so from other periods of Bollywood cinema too—from the music of the famous seventies' music director Rahul Dev Burman, to a quote on villains and heroes from *Sholay*, to contemporary 'bullet time' action sequences from the film *The Matrix*. *The Matrix* set a trend in action aesthetics that was to be repeated exhaustively time after time in commercial Western cinema that was possible as part of the machination and assemblage of Hollywood cinema's strive for mega profits from mega budgets and to reiterate its visual power as the centre of filmdom. *Main Hoon Na* following in such footsteps as the epicentre of Indian filmdom also sought to achieve a landmark profit from a huge investment and to set new standards in Hindi cinema action aesthetics. Yet, when the 'bullet time' action sequence is used in *Main Hoon Na* directly to quote a scene from *The Matrix* it does so by alluding to the use of visual effects from Hollywood as a sign of mimicry. In *The Matrix* Neo (Keanu Reeves) falls back and bends at his knees in an extreme L-shape posture whilst bullets are fired at him by an agent of the matrix. This scene is replicated in a comic mode in *Main Hoon Na* when Ram (Shahrukh Khan) falls back not to dodge bullets but to avoid globules of spit that are projected at him from the mouth of a shouting physics professor in the staff room (see Figure 6.2). This quotation is not only recognised by urban Indian and diasporic audiences who have seen *The Matrix* but is also registered for Indian audiences who might not be familiar with the Hollywood source. A teacher of Hindi who cannot speak English properly, Mrs Kakkad (Bindu), asks one of her colleagues

Figure 6.2: Shahrukh Khan mimics Neo's (Keanu Reeves) fall from *The Matrix* through a bullet time action sequence to dodge spit balls fired from the mouth of his physics professor in the film *Main Hoon Na*

'Hey, this was in the 'Matrick'?' to which her bemused co-teacher replies 'You mean *The Matrix*?' This source of mimicry references the visual possibilities engendered by Hollywood cinema, itself inspired by the aesthetics of Hong Kong action cinema, as a display of technical wizardry and ocular amazement that sets a new standard in Hindi action cinema, but also with a tongue-in-cheek gesture that nods at Bollywood audiences' recognition of this moment as a play with quotations from Hollywood cinema. In this way the conventions of mimicry, coupled in this instance with humour, serve to illustrate and dismantle textual power relations as one way from Hollywood to Bollywood, or from the West to the East, and allow audiences a space in which to marvel and mock at the characters and themselves as a simultaneous and double articulation.

The issue, then, of how Bollywood cinema allegedly copies from Hollywood is not as straightforward as is suggested by some. This view is further complexified when we consider that, of late, Hollywood has also been borrowing from Bollywood cinema itself, as seen in the song and dance aesthetics of Baz Luhrman's *Moulin Rouge* (2003),[2] or as seen in Reese Witherspoon's rendition of a nineteenth-century British ballroom dance stylised through Bollywood steps in Mira Nair's *Vanity Fair* (2004), and choreographed by one of Bollywood's leading choreographers Farah Khan.

CO-PRODUCTIONS AND BOLLYWOOD

The use of referents from Hollywood cinema by Bollywood cinema and vice versa, is a complex area and needs to be situated within the context of the globalisation of film wherein production techniques, finance and aesthetic sources are increasingly being brought into contact with each other from different parts of the same production centres as well as from around the world. In particular, the granting of official 'industry status' to Bollywood cinema in May 1998 has led to the liberalisation of its film industry and has opened up possibilities for co-productions via new sources of income both in and beyond India. Until this time, finance for the production of Bollywood movies came from independent producers and directors, business entrepreneurs attracted by the glamour of the entertainment industries, kith and kin networks from within the film industry, or even, as has been widely alleged, through money related to the criminal underworld (on the history of Bollywood's lead up to official film industry status, see Ganti 2004: 43–52). The status of commercial film-making in India has moved from being perceived as a producer of vice by successive governments since Indian independence (leading to the imposition of high taxes), to being liberalised in the late nineties, thereby allowing it to benefit from actual rewards in the form of lower production charges, tax benefits, and for film-makers to accumulate production finance from banks and other corporate financial institutions. The industry has thus been accorded an important and legitimate economic and symbolic status, supported and developed as a marker of Indian success in the international marketplace of goods where Bollywood films compete with Hollywood ones at box offices around the world.

However, since the announcement of Bollywood as an official industry and granting it liberalisation, film-makers have been divided on whether financing from banks and other corporate institutions is a truly productive venture. Press reports from the national and international Indian media (see, for example, Unnikrishnan and Shah 2003) have indicated a discord at national conventions in India that have brought together film-makers, corporate managers and trade and entertainment ministers to discuss the possible future for financing in the cinema industry. Financial institutions consider film-making, and in particular popular Hindi film-making, as very risky business given the number of high failure to low success ratios of films at the box office. Subsequently, funding from financial institutions comes with a number of conditions attached. Banks and financial institutions have asked the film industry to form a corporate culture akin to professional businesses and to prepare bankable scripts in order to get funding. The unorganised and high-risk nature of the film industry, where often no date is set for completion on most films before production commences and where fiscal losses are very high, has made corporate financiers nervous about releasing capital. Corporate financiers are more in favour of risk formula assessments in order to guard against potential losses to their investments and are seeking what they consider 'safe' investment ventures such as television channels and exhibition infrastructures like the growing number of multiplex cinemas across urban India which have predictable cash flows. Film merchandising and product endorsements (for example, Pepsi and Coca-Cola) along the lines of indirect advertising inherent in contemporary Hollywood cinema is also being encouraged as additional revenue for films, thereby allowing corporate financiers such as banks to be more comfortable about venturing into debt financing for film-makers.

Such demands have met with mixed responses from the film-makers themselves. On the one hand there is the view by some that the entertainment business is one of individuality and ad hoc collaborative creativity. Film-makers such as Shekhar Kapur and Yash Chopra have gone on record claiming that the corporatisation of film-making will damage the creative culture of commercial film-making in India, and that to accord this cultural production as a higher risk than any other business is a false alarm. While on the other hand, film-makers such as Shyam Benegal and Mani Ratnam favour funding by corporate institutions and banks. They believe that this will lead to new routes for funding in terms of co-production possibilities (Unnikrishnan and Shah 2003). It appears then that a debate is in motion amongst film-makers, financiers and the state regarding whether or not to keep film-making as a flexible creative activity or manage that creativity alongside enterprise governance.

Furthermore, the Indian government, urged on by Indian film and media production companies, is seeking to formalise co-production treaties with other countries such as Britain, Italy and Canada (Shah 2003). Indian media production companies are exploring co-production with foreign and transnational media companies as new avenues for funding and joint ventures. Indian producers are keen to market their films with crossover appeal amongst international audiences with an eye on maximising their profits and this makes co-production treaties with other countries all the more important. With co-production treaties companies can explore the advantage of hiring foreign talent and using their technology to make quality films at competitive costs and be able to market and distribute them globally. The move towards securing co-production treaties can be further understood in the context of the fast growing Indian media sectors and amidst the expansion of South Asian consumer culture in recent years that has also caught the attention of global media companies and foreign investors to the subcontinent.

It is amidst these changes in the globalisation of the Indian film industry that the actualisation of production and venture alliances has been taking place that suggests the following social possibilities. For example, the past few years have seen a number of big budget films being co-produced. In one particular instance, India-based Pritish Nandy Communications, teamed up with US-based diasporic venture capitalists and film enthusiasts Raju Patel's Film Club to generate joint funding for the film *Kaante* (Thorns, dir. Sanjay Gupta, 2002). This crime drama, based around the aftermath of a bloody bank robbery gone wrong, was shot predominantly in Los Angeles with a big star cast from Bollywood headed by Amitabh Bachchan. The film comprised high production values and a tight script that borrowed and reworked episodes from other Hollywood films like *Heat, Reservoir Dogs* and *The Usual Suspects*. Such diasporic alliances between Nandy Communications and Patel's Film Club have been formalised and made professional in the post-industry status of Bollywood cinema. Whereas previously such overseas investments by diasporic Indians was perhaps more for the glamour aspect of being associated with making films and the chance for a one-off colossal profit if the film went on to become a blockbuster, co-productions allow the coming together of local and global individuals, groups and corporate film-makers to share economic and creative responsibilities and risks and any ensuing profits (see Sen and Anusha 2003).

Ek Hasina Thi (There was a Beautiful Girl, dir. Sriram Raghavan, 2004), a story of a young woman, Sarika (Urmila Matondkar), who enacts her revenge on her lover, Karan (Saif Ali Khan), after being used and imprisoned for his criminal activities, is the first major co-production with a Hollywood entertainment house—20th Century Fox. This gritty and dark feminist tale, also co-produced with Bollywood's Ram Gopal Verma who has made a name for himself by making films that play with and subvert the conventional romantic genre, was a bold step taken by Fox as its maiden venture into co-production. Previously, Hollywood production houses have only been interested in investing in the distribution of films, in the setting up of multiplexes, or in the purchase of equity in television channels that have been deemed as safe investments. With Fox's venture into actual film-making it remains to be seen whether others will also follow and what implications this might have for the creative production of Bollywood films in terms of themes and content.[3]

The move of foreign media companies and capital to India demonstrates the possibilities that the globalisation of film brings with it. In one such example, a US-based digital studio company West Wing Studios has moved some of its operations from Florida to Goa. Benefiting from the cheaper running and labour costs in India as compared to the US, it aims to finance two low budget Hollywood movies and to digitally enhance and colour 40 classic black and white Bollywood films, as well as to colour original black and white films for Sony Pictures and 20th Century Fox (D'Mello 2003). However, the relocation of operations from foreign-based media companies to India sets off a wider debate in the globalisation of economics and the circulation of cultural goods about who benefits from the outsourcing of finances to other parts of the world—where labour, materials and running costs are cheaper—and who loses out. The globalisation of media production in the era of international liberalisation has seen traditional geo-economic regions, such as Europe and the US, being realigned in terms of economic growth and symbolic power. Nonetheless, it remains uncertain as to what investment opportunities the movement of capital and operations from the traditional colonial geo-economic bases in the West to parts of the developing and former colonised world, such as India, will amount to. Is the movement of such capital and operations from one part of the globe to another simply an opportunity to make more profits? Or, is it possible to spread economic development across both traditional geo-economic regions and new investment places in a sustained and equitable manner? Cinema industries and films are increasingly becoming a part of this nexus of the global movement of media companies and capital.

Post-industry status Bollywood has also seen the mobilisation of Indian producers, directors and film companies setting up bases across global frontiers in order to maximise their profits from distribution (Padmanabhan 2004). Previously, distribution was in the hands of a few enterprising individuals around the world who charged a large proportion of the profits from box-office takings. It was also alleged by film-makers that distributors often operated in a less than transparent system when taking their share of the revenue. Since 1998, the big names in Bollywood cinema production have been active, setting up their own bases abroad to deal with key overseas distribution territories directly. These include Yash Raj Films (of *Dilwale Dulhaniya Le Jayenge* and *Veer Zaara* fame), UTV Communications (*Fiza*, *Lakshya* and *Swades*), and Zee Telefilms Ltd (*Gadar-Ek Prem Katha*), who now have offices in London and in New York to deal with European and North American markets respectively. Since interacting with distribution networks in these countries Bollywood film-makers have learnt to adapt some of Hollywood's film distribution and promotion activities to their own films—such as increased expenditure on publicity and international advertising—in order to increase their exposure amongst international audiences. This has seen the creation of Bollywood movie trailers with simultaneous third person narrative voiceovers and subtitles in English shown in selected mainstream cinema theatres and also appearing on Western rental DVDs and videos. Large advertisement hoardings of Bollywood movies have also started to appear in major multicultural cities in the UK, and even Bollywood billposters have been advertising on the tube in London. Even Blockbuster, the transnational media rental chain store, spurred by the increasing global visibility of Bollywood films and popular culture has started to stock Bollywood film titles in some of its stores and also as part of its on-line rental catalogues in the UK and in the US. These activities, then, suggest the arrival of popular Hindi cinema on the international entertainment and media landscapes in ways that have yet to be fully charted. At one level this arrival has been possible through the work of Indian film-makers and their corporate allies as intervening in the liberalising international sphere of film-making, distribution and exhibition, with an eye on maximising the financial returns for their cultural production efforts. On another level, Bollywood is seen as a market gap among current services to be exploited by transnational media rental outlets. And at another level still, and echoing the sentiments of Bollywood cinema goers in Chapter 4 and of the Western commodification of Bollywood popular culture in Chapter 5, diasporic South Asian audiences are mediating their way through deciphering Bollywood as the new chic and cool, and simultaneously to mark their own settlements, arrival and affinities with popular Hindi films through these same global conduits of Bollywood cinema's circulation.

Figure 6.3: Bollywood cinema on the landscape of Western multicultural cities: A film poster of *Veer Zaara* (dir. Yash Chopra, 2004) being advertised on large billboards alongside Western adverts in the city of Birmingham, UK (personal photograph)

Another important area to consider post-industry status is the possibility of recent Bollywood cinema as playing a viable part in the momentum for peace initiatives and cross-border alliances between warring nations India and Pakistan. Both nations have been at war, on and off, since 1947—the period of independence from colonial rule and violent partition from each other. Officially, Bollywood films have been banned in Pakistani cinema halls, and vice versa, for decades by successive governments due to the political sensitivities and on and off economic and cultural relations during war and peace between the two countries. However, through piracy video routes and through cable and satellite means, Bollywood films have always been a part of Pakistani popular culture, amassing millions of audiences and followers. It has also been reported that Bollywood films have been shown 'unofficially' for a long time in cinemas in major Pakistani cities (Dubey 2003).[4] Moreover, in recent years it has been documented that Pakistani film-makers have been making trips to India 'quietly' under the guise of visiting friends but in reality to network with and hire Indian film-making talent to work on Pakistani feature films (Misra 2003). When Pakistanis cannot get over to India, Indian film workers are hired to travel and work in Switzerland, Spain, Mauritius and West Asia as a way of getting around visa problems and state tensions between the two countries. While Pakistani actors and actresses have worked and been popular in Bollywood films for some years now—Salma Agha in *Nikaah* (Wedding, dir. B.R. Chopra, 1982) and Zeba Bakhtiar in *Henna* (Henna, 1991)—the Indian contribution to Pakistani film-making goes officially uncredited. Pakistani actor-director and co-producer Javed Sheikh made *Yeh Dil Aap Ka Huwa* (This Heart is Yours, 2003) using technicians and singers from Bollywood. To date this film is the most expensive film made in Pakistan set in foreign locations and with high production values akin to Bollywood blockbusters. It proved highly successful at the Pakistan box-office raking in record profits but with its Indian input unsourced (Dubey 2003).

All this could change as a result of the peace effort being made by both sides, as India and Pakistan strive to formalise the screening of Bollywood films in Pakistani cinemas, albeit subject to censorship, in an ongoing attempt to establish better formal trade and finance relations and also improve the state of Pakistani cinemas that have been decreasing in numbers (Adarsh 2004). The opening of dialogue and political doors for free trade between India and Pakistan could also lead to Bollywood films being accorded a legitimate cultural status within Pakistan and promote cross-border co-production possibilities between Pakistani and Indian producers and directors. Pakistan in particular could begin to formally look to India to draw from its film-making talent rather than to go to the West as it has done in the past and thereby save on production costs. Veteran Bollywood director and producer Mahesh Bhatt has gone on record declaring that it's time to do business 'legally and openly' between the two film-making nations to each other's benefit (Dubey 2003). At a thematic and representational level too, there has been a bold move of late to directly address the divisive chasms and possibilities for peace between the two nations in recent big budget Bollywood films such as *Pinjar* (2003), *Main Hoon Na* (dir. Farah Khan, 2004), *Veer Zaara* (dir. Yash Chopra, 2004) and *Ab Tumhare Hawale Watan Saathiyo* (dir. Anil Sharma, 2004).

Some British Asians are also attempting to partake in celluloid diplomacy and contribute to the peace process between the two countries by funding and making films advocating the need for dialogue between India and Pakistan. In this respect, in the north of England, Huddersfield-based Afzal Khan's Paragon Pictures, a British registered company, is keen to finance and make films that draw on film-making talents from both countries. Paragon's second film *Larki Punjaban* (Punjabi Girl, 2003) is a story of a Sikh–Muslim love affair that was reported as doing well at international box offices. Furthermore, with its films branded as being British, Paragon Pictures is able to exhibit movies in cinema screens in both India and Pakistan without getting caught in any political wrangles when each country refuses to show films from the other's cinemas (Branigan 2004).

Developments on the Indian and global co-production front, then, with the globalisation of Bollywood cinema and films, offers a range of social outcomes that are in need of further observation and comment to ascertain where they lead in actual terms. Furthermore, with the synergies and possibilities that are available in the coming together of mainstream Bollywood and Hollywood film-making aesthetics and practices, we can also look towards the developing work of South Asian diasporic film-makers and to some of their films for further analysis.

BOLLYWOOD IN THE FILMS OF SOUTH ASIAN DIASPORIC FILM-MAKERS

Jigna Desai (2004) in her exploration of South Asian diasporic film-makers who draw on the aesthetics and film-making practices of both

Bollywood and Hollywood cinemas considers the cultural politics of their films. Drawing on Mikhail Bakhtin's notion of heteroglossia (the multiple speech and language types available in popular cultural texts), she considers the distinctiveness of these films as characterised by their aesthetic polyvocality. South Asian diasporic films are seen to be located 'between' and 'beyond' Hollywood and Bollywood cinemas, intervening against the idea of national cinemas as essentialist projects (Desai 2004: 36).

South Asian diasporic centred films that have achieved mainstream exposure and feature aesthetics from Bollywood cinema include, amongst others, *Bhaji on the Beach* (dir. Gurinder Chadha, 1993), *East is East* (dir. Damien O'Donnell, 1999), *Bollywood Calling* (dir. Nagesh Kukunoor, 2001), *Monsoon Wedding* (dir. Mira Nair 2002), *Bollywood/Hollywood* (dir. Deepa Mehta, 2002) and *Bride and Prejudice* (dir. Gurinder Chadha, 2004).[5] The success of recent films by Deepa Mehta, Gurinder Chadha and Mira Nair in particular have been discussed as attempts to present a feminist reckoning of South Asian diasporic cultural production and politics (see ibid.: Chapter 8). Gurinder Chadha, for example, has often been quoted in interviews as using her films as well as her film-making practices as an expression of her angst towards an ethnocentric worldview (Bailey-Grant 2004; Bhattacharyya and Gabriel 1994).

The ensuing analysis of the deployment of Bollywood aesthetics in episodes from select films from the aforementioned diasporic filmmakers is offered to consider the social and aesthetic effects of and changes to Bollywood cinema as it is used to articulate some of the cultural politics of these films, and thereby to consider the sociological insights offered by these films. An attempt is made to consider the cultural and social possibilities of 'meaning making' that these films engender through an analysis of some of their key moments as they articulate with wider social and cultural concerns.

Bhaji on the Beach

Bhaji on the Beach depicts the story of a British South Asian women's group from Birmingham on their day trip to Blackpool. Desai (2004: Chapter 5) appropriately interprets this film as contemplating the possibility of women's agency through social mobility both within a patriarchal domestic sphere and a public sphere of tourism, leisure and constructed escapism at Blackpool beach. Desai uses the metaphors of 'homesickness' and 'motion sickness' as arising out of feminist studies about gendered embodied subjectivities to describe a feeling of movement—social, actual and psychological—of the female protagonists that shift between the setting of the home and the desire to be elsewhere too. The amalgamation of Bollywood aesthetics in *Bhaji on the Beach* serve to play out the concerns of the film, primarily of how the women negotiate their place in their different settings, their temporary escape from their family lives, and their personal desires based around gendered and sexual pleasures.

Asha (Lalitha Ahmed), for instance, is a middle-aged housewife who dutifully prays every morning, runs the family newspaper shop, and attends to the needs of her demanding family. Before leaving for Blackpool (and whilst she is there) Asha is seen contemplating and hallucinating her many dilemmas—of the life that she finds herself in, of the life that she has chosen for herself, and of what could have been or might be. In Blackpool Asha is romantically pursued by Ambrose (Peter Cellier), who on appearance is an English gentleman who is courteous and charming in his mannerisms. In one of her dreams, Asha imagines herself with Ambrose in an idyllic park setting that is laden with beautiful trees and flowers. Both Asha and Ambrose are dressed in signifiers of South Asian dress—Asha in a sari and Ambrose in a kurta and pyjama with a waistcoat. They are seen performing a serenade-style song and dance sequence with accompanying music, as if from a romantic Bollywood film. This is Asha's fantasy of sexual desire and romantic escape with Ambrose as her possible suitor. However, this dream is only momentarily lived as, also in Bollywood mode, it starts to rain and before the sequence becomes an intimate 'wet sari scene' wherein Asha reveals herself to her partner through titillation, Ambrose's brown face starts to wash away and uncovers his white skin. Asha is awoken abruptly to the realisation that Ambrose is a white man with an orientalist sexual fantasy to rescue Asian women whom he considers to be oppressed by their own cultures. The insertion of Bollywood aesthetics in this segment of the film draw us into the imagination of Asha to enter into her dream world where she is able to fantasise another possibility. However, this possibility is placed within a context of social, racial and sexual power relations that suggest that neither Asha nor Ambrose are suited for each other. The scene becomes part comic and part social commentary as the characters are seen to be performing the Bollywood romantic chase as a clichéd 'singing and dancing around trees' rendition that is deliberately kitsch and not quite right.

East is East

East is East is set in seventies Salford, in the north west of England. George Khan (Om Puri), a British Pakistani, and his white-English wife Ella Khan (Linda Bassett) run a fish and chips shop for their living, whilst parenting their seven children who are at a cross-roads in terms of race and culture: belonging to mixed race parents and coming of age at the dawn of a multiracial post-war British society, where social transformation collide with right-wing Enoch Powell-esque politics. *East is East* was one of the overall top-grossing films in Britain during 1999, earning more than £7 million at the box office (Desai 2004: 50). Loretta Collins Klobah (2003) reads the film—as an attempt by its writer, British Asian Ayub Khan-Din—and the media frenzy surrounding the success of the film at the British box office as a celebratory moment of multiculturalism. However, as Klobah alerts us, the construction of multiculturalism present in the film and around its box-office success is accredited to both the implicit and explicit references to 'otherness' that are given heightened illustration through the character of George Khan. George offers audiences the possibilities of comedy and tragedy based around notions of his Pakistani- and Muslim-Englishness. George is depicted as a staunch patriarch and harsh disciplinarian whenever he takes decisions to direct his family into a way of life that he feels will suit them best— a conservative and reactionary Muslim and English working-class upbringing that is responding to the socio-cultural changes in seventies Britain. As such, he is often at odds, and at times literally in direct violent confrontation, with his wife and children as they move towards an attempt at reconciling their different cultural outlooks.

The Bollywood aesthetics in this film are used as a mediating device between the two worlds existing in the diegesis of the text, those of East and West. Bollywood films and popular culture are shown to play a small yet important cultural role in the lives of the Khans. The family dress up and go out together to watch a film at the Moti Mahal cinema in Bradford that is owned by a cousin. George sings romantically to Ella in the dark cinema auditorium over the title song from the sixties film *Chaudhvin Ka Chand* (dir. M. Sadiq, 1960) affirming his love to her, whilst also personally registering a moment from his youth. For the children, especially the two young adult males Tariq (Jimi Mistry) and Abdul (Raji James), the Bollywood films provide a world of make believe that is part-familiar and part-alien to them, but nonetheless a part of who they are. They watch the screen with wry smiles and adoration simultaneously.

In an earlier scene, the only daughter of the family, the feisty Meenah (Archie Punjabi) is seen helping her brother Abdul in their back yard preparing some fish for sale in their shop. They have a radio on in the background, over which a Bollywood film song, 'Inhe logon ne' (These very people) from the 1971 film *Pakeezah* (Pure Heart, dir. Kamal Amrohi, 1971) starts to play. In *Pakeezah* this song is sung on-screen by actress Meena Kumari, who plays the role of a prostitute with a good heart, and who teases the men in her brothel through her singing and dancing. The song is a playful critique of society, addressing men in terms of social class. It refers to men who often privately frequent courtesans by night and also lead respectable public lives during the day. Meenah starts to mimic this song and performs a dance of her own. She is dressed in a worker's white overall and has a broom in hand which she uses as a stand-in dancing partner. She moves around the back yard in playful and part-defiant gestures and goes over to her brother Abdul, drapes a work cloth over her head as if wearing a *dupatta* (head scarf) and teases him (see Figure 6.4). This redeployment of the original Bollywood song is used to demonstrate how the Khan children, and Meenah in particular, view and use the Bollywood referents in their lives. The original song itself is a critique on the use of women by men and men's alleged respectability. Meenah transplants this meaning through dance and mimicry in her everyday northern British life of the seventies where she and her brothers are trying to negotiate a liberal upbringing in working-class Salford amidst the concerns and demands of their conservative Muslim father. Furthermore, she makes this song and dance her own as an expression of the inequities of gender in a predominantly male working-class culture through the free and abrupt movements of her body that profess a desire of wanting to be elsewhere.

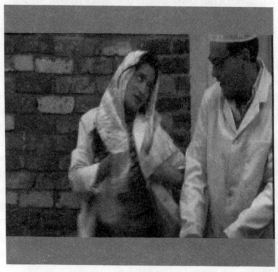

Figure 6.4: Meenah dances to a Bollywood song and teases her brother Abdul as a play on social relations and as a gesture to be somewhere else in the film *East is East*

Bend it Like Beckham

In *Bend it Like Beckham* Gurinder Chadha draws on a range of cultural referents from contemporary Britain, including British pop, bhangra, Bollywood, and UK black fusion music genres, to elaborate on the story of her main protagonist Jesminder/Jess Bhamra (Parminder Nagra). Jess wants to make it as a female soccer player and also becomes involved in a multiracial heterosexual romance. Jess also has to convince her family, especially her domineering matriarchal mother who wants nothing more than for Jess to settle down to a suitable arranged marriage, that she has a genuine ambition for the game and to bring them on her side. The film is primarily a heterosexual romance narrative infused with a feminist focus on female sexual agency that is supported by a queer subplot in the film. Jess's male best friend Tony (Amit Chana) comes out to her as gay and seeks her acceptance of his sexuality amidst his fears of a wider homophobic culture, and Jess's relationship with her football team mate, Juliette (Keira Knightley), is wrongly interpreted as a lesbian one by Jess's relatives and Juliette's mother. Desai considers the film as an attempt to disrupt South Asian gender normativities of heterosexuality through challenging the dominant gendered ideologies such as female chastity and virginity, multiracial romance, and arranged marriages. Desai further suggests that the popularity of this film, being hugely successful at both the British and US box-offices, is based on the accessibility and familiarity of these narratives to crossover viewers. Non-South Asian viewers may find these challenges not only non-threatening but also familiar and comfortable (Desai 2004: 214). The use of Bollywood referents alongside a diverse UK fusion popular culture aims to progress the emotions of the characters in the film.

Jess meets and gradually falls in love with her football coach Joe (Jonathan Rhys-Meyers). During their separation the background music that underscores their longing for each other is the track 'Tera bina nahin lagda' (I am restless without you) by the late *qawwali* singer Nusrat Fateh Ali Khan, that has been remixed by British Asian music producer Bally Sagoo as a romantic Bollywood ballad. The scene of Jess and Joe's parting is edited alongside the pain of separation facing Jess's older sister whose wedding has been called off by her fiancé's parents, and is also juxtaposed with the scene of Jess's parents consoling each other after the realisation that their daughter is serious about playing football. In this way the same piece of Bollywood music is used to connect across the related emotions and social trials of different characters in the film. The use of Bollywood-remixed music signifies the personal sensibilities of protagonists, both South Asian and white.

Bride and Prejudice

In her more recent film *Bride and Prejudice* (2004), Gurinder Chadha remakes the story of Jane Austen's novel *Pride and Prejudice* and relocates it to the city of Amritsar in Punjab, northwest India. The idea of families arranging mutually beneficial status marriages translates smoothly to its new setting—nineteenth-century Hertfordshire's unmarried Bennet sisters and meddling mother become the lower middle-class Bakshis from contemporary Amritsar. The suitors Bingley and Darcy are respectively a second-generation British Asian (Naveen Andrews) and a wealthy American hotelier (Martin Henderson), while the cunning Wickham (Daniel Gillies) is an English backpacker looking for his next exotic fling. The lead character Lalitha Bakshi (Austen's Elizabeth Bennet) is played by former Miss World and current leading Bollywood actress, Aishwarya Rai.

With *Bride and Prejudice*, Chadha creates this text in a predominantly Bollywood mould, more so than her previous films, and also uses aesthetics from Black British film-making practices and also from mainstream Hollywood.[6] Chadha acknowledges that building on the success of her film *Bend it Like Beckham*, *Bride and Prejudice* is more of an explicit attempt at a crossover film that pays homage to her varied influences as a film-maker. She is very keen to do away with much of the uninformed populist criticisms often levelled at Bollywood cinema and the exaggerated focus on kitsch in the Western media, and has spoken in her many media interviews around the launch of the film in October 2004, of the challenges and fusion possibilities of bringing together at least three different film-making languages in this film:

> It was three different worlds coming together .... That's also why I chose to do it now, because I felt Bollywood was being hijacked in a particular way .... People were focusing on the

really kitsch side of it. Yes there is a lot of kitsch and it is formula, but at the same time there's a wonderful purity of emotion and a lot about it that's brilliant. I wanted to do something that paid homage to some of the films that were very much part of who I was as a film-maker. (Gurinder Chadha interviewed by Leigh Singer, 'Mix and Match', *The Times*, Screen Section, 7 October 2004, p. 14.)

The Bollywood aesthetics are central to this movie in terms of its camera work, song and dance routines (both in Hindi and in English), dialogues, melodrama, grand colourful sets, and lavish outdoor location shots spanning Amritsar, Goa, London and Los Angeles. Through these, *Bride and Prejudice* covers similar thematic subjects as in Chadha's previous films: heterosexual romance, female agency amidst conservative and often patriarchal cultures, and the exoticisation of Asian women in the global commodified marketplace. More globally, these aesthetics are also used to suggest to international audiences, i.e., to non-South Asians and South Asians, that although the cultural registers and nuances in how different people express themselves might be different, often the grand and important messages, of the pursuit of love for instance, are not that dissimilarly expressed.

For example, towards the film's climax before Lalitha and Darcy try to come to terms with their differences and announce their love for each other, they have to rescue Lalitha's youngest sister Lucky (Peeya Chowdhary) who has been lured away by Wickham in order for him to seduce her. They follow and chase them across London's canals, its Millennium Eye, and catch up with them in a cinema hall that is showing a classic seventies Bollywood film *Purab aur Paschim* (East and West, dir. Manoj Kumar, 1970) with a predominantly British Asian audience watching. *Purab aur Paschim* is essentially a conservative tale, advocating the need to not forget one's Indian cultural identity and the dangers of the hedonist and promiscuous West during immediate post-war migration to Britain. Darcy and Wickham explode on to the stage in front of the screen and start to fight with one another. This is precisely at the moment when on-screen in the cinema, the film's lead Manoj Kumar is rescuing the heroine, Saira Bano, from being raped by the villain played by Prem Chopra and they also start to fight. The diegesis of *Bride and Prejudice* meets with and coalesces alongside the diegesis of *Purab aur Paschim*. The audience in the cinema hall are at first disgruntled that their viewing experience has been disturbed but then are equally captivated by the actions of Lalitha, Lucky, Darcy and Wickham. The two diegeses are interspersed with each other as we see punches thrown by the two heroes and villains from both screen worlds. Both the heroes, from *Bride and Prejudice* and *Purab aur Paschim*, overcome their villains and rescue the girl. In *Bride and Prejudice*, upon learning his seductive intentions, Lucky ends her liaison with Wickham by slapping him, much to the audiences' approval in the cinema hall. In this way *Bride and Prejudice* emphasises its feminist message whilst using the aesthetics of Bollywood from *Purab aur Paschim* to be taken a step further. In *Purab aur Paschim* it is the male lead who rescues and restores the heroine's honour in the seventies, and in *Bride and Prejudice* the hero again battles with the villain; yet in order to save the heroine's honour two cultures join forces, with the additional last word and action blow given by a female character in the contemporary present. Through homage, then, Bollywood as a cultural history and resource is acknowledged in *Bride and Prejudice* and is also adapted and remoulded to fit the needs of the present. Further still, the use of Bollywood in *Bride and Prejudice* features not only at an aesthetic level but also explicitly announces its arrival on the stage of global film-making as one possible source among others from which to work.

In *Bhaji on the Beach*, then, there is deliberate use of Bollywood as exaggerated kitsch to suggest the not quite right; in *East is East* Bollywood signifiers act as mediating devices between different cultural worlds; in *Bend it Like Beckham* remixed Bollywood musical sources profess the varied sensibilities and emotions of its multicultural characters; and in *Bride and Prejudice* Bollywood is paid homage to and amalgamated comfortably with other film-making genres. In these selected examples, as well as from other films mentioned earlier, the use of Bollywood aesthetics as part of diasporic film-making practices in the UK and in the US are being developed to represent fluid images of, and to depict eclectic narratives about, its characters, not least its South Asian protagonists. The Bollywood referents are also being adapted and translated as part of a fusion of different cinematic traditions and styles of film-making that are able to draw on and make a number of social commentaries.

If these aforementioned examples suggest the development of Bollywood film aesthetics and their ensuing social commentaries as part of a trajectory of over a decade of South Asian diasporic film-making and cultural change that has culminated in the contemporary moment as a marker of arrival in the landscape of international film, then we also need to situate another use of Bollywood aesthetics that sits alongside these films as also reminding us of the menacing familiar tropes of representations that South Asians have been historically marked by in Western cinemas.

The Guru (2002) directed by Daisy Von Sherler Mayer, co-produced with money from the UK, France and the USA, and promoted and distributed by United International Picture's (UIP) around the world, is an example of mainstream white Western interpretations of the East as exotic and stereotypically orientalist (Said 1978). Made and released during the discovery of Bollywood by the Western entertainment and cultural industries in 2002, *The Guru*, billed as a romantic comedy, follows the story of Ramu Gupta (Jimi Mistry) who leaves Mumbai to go to the US to become a star actor. Instead, he auditions for a role in a porn movie before going on to masquerade as a sex guru to New York's disenchanted and rich white Americans. Ramu meets and falls in love with his co-porn actress Sharonna (Heather Graham), who coaches him in her theories of liberal sexuality that he passes off as acquired wisdom from India.

The use of Bollywood aesthetics in this film are used as a backdrop for fun and humour through orientalist representations of India and the East more generally, as serving a purpose to fulfil the needs of white Westerners. Whilst there is a well-intentioned attempt at rendering a Hollywood track in the guise of a Bollywood song and dance sequence—Ramu and Sharonna announce their love for each other dressed up in traditional South Asian attire and dancing Bollywood steps to the music and lyrics of the song 'You're the one that I want' from the film *Grease*—this is an exceptional moment in the film as it is set into context amidst a plethora of images and representations that cast South Asians and other minorities in the US in predominantly subservient roles with exaggerated thick accents. The ethnic minorities in the film are either struggling as domestic servants or restaurant workers who often experience racism and prejudice from white people. There are overt uses of sitars and *tablas* throughout the film signifying Indian characters in the US as foreign immigrants, and a clichéd idea of the East and its people is generalised as pure and innocent through the effeminised and naive

Ramu. When Ramu dons his guise as a sex guru, the East is made further exotic and sexually appealing to White westerners through Ramu's Kama Sutra style sexual-spiritual sermons. *The Guru*, then, seeks to cash in on the international exposure and hype surrounding Bollywood cinema and popular culture and does little more than to reaffirm longstanding stereotypes about South Asians and cultural representations of the East more widely.

CONCLUSION

Sociology has been to the movies. An attempt has been made through socio-cultural and aesthetic analyses to consider some aspects of the cinema of Bollywood in terms of its films, its workings as an industry, and its popular culture and its audiences in order to draw out and understand its generating of possible pleasures, desires, social processes, and its role in the formation of cultural politics.

The sociology that has been advocated and demonstrated throughout this book has been one that has little to do with following the canonical figures and classical theories of the discipline in a systemic and exhaustive manner, and more to do with demonstrating a practicing of the sociological imagination as it is brought into dialogue with studies of the cinema, namely from the related disciplines of film, media and cultural studies. A conscious effort has been made to revive a sociological interest in cinema and in films through the case study of Bollywood cinema by applying theoretical frameworks and methodological tools that can be seen as germane to these different subject areas. By drawing on the methods of qualitative interviews and participant observation an attempt has been made to elaborate on and give a textured feeling to some of the films being discussed, to the film cultures of cinema going, and also to the translations of Bollywood songs, music and dancing in queer diasporic spaces. In this way an attempt has been made to argue for the need to think imaginatively about the circulation of cinema as a global industry, films as popular cultural texts, and the relationships that are possible between cinema and its audiences. By taking sociology to the cinema, and vice versa, it has been argued that we need to look at the range of intellectual and interdisciplinary possibilities that are available to us as cultural and social researchers in order to renew a dialogue between sociology and studies of the cinema, thereby restimulating the possibilities of how we might be able to think creatively about sociology and cinema. What one hopes has emerged is a genuine example of doing sociologically-informed research alongside questions of social representations and the importance of deciphering cultural texts through close analysis. In this vein, then, the main findings and arguments of this book have been as follows:

In Chapter 2 the importance of the production and picturisation of film songs and music in Bollywood cinema has been used as a way to consider the cinema's eclectic aesthetic composition as drawing on a range of South Asian, Western and other musical sources. Film songs have also been shown to be central to the production process of Bollywood films as almost always being the first sequences of the film to be shot in order to secure further funding. The collaborative input of music directors, musicians, playback artists and star performers is crucial to the successful picturisation of the songs. The songs also act as narrative accelerators and as a step beyond the immediate narrative that incorporate some of the key thematic issues that recur in Bollywood cinema. In the analysis of the film *Hum Aap Kain Hain Kaun..!*, the depiction of love and romance, and an engagement with issues of tradition and modernity have been paid attention to; and also in the readings of the films *Fiza* and *Chalte Chalte*, the social representations of class and of social minorities has been offered. Bollywood cinema ostensibly makes a space for the culturally hegemonic ruling class, i.e., more often than not middle-class Hindu Indians, but that space is left open and problematised by the cinema itself and by its audiences through the inclusion of characters and representations that are deemed as 'minorities'. Bollywood film songs as narrative devices, operationalised through the use of spectacle, are part and parcel of this cultural contestation.

Chapter 3 offered an analysis of the film *Pardes* as an example of a contemporary Bollywood film that engaged with diasporic issues through the lens of Bollywood cinema. The chapter drew on qualitative interview research about the film that was conducted with actual diasporic British South Asian audiences. My respondents' own readings of the audio-visual signs of the film, as interpreted by myself and my own further elaborations of the film, sought to provide a dialogic assessment of *Pardes* by amalgamating text-based readings with audience response. My respondents made sense of the film as containing elements of reality, fantasy and their articulations, as coming together to offer them a flexible understanding and construction of their diasporic sensibilities and familial connections in Britain, South Asia and elsewhere. Bollywood films in Britain, as in the example of *Pardes*, offers those diasporic South Asians that partake in its activities a wider set of representations and possible lives than those offered in mainstream Western cinema. The chapter also offered a reading of the performances of urban Indian and diasporic identity through a case study of the actor Shahrukh Khan as a contemporary 'star' in Bollywood cinema's circulation amidst cultural globalisation. Taken together, these two sections suggest that the role and representations of urban India and the diaspora in recent Bollywood cinema are constructed through Bollywood cinema's imagined and often conservative understanding of the relationship between the homeland and the diaspora and hence is a refraction of that real relationship. Bollywood cinema constructs urban India and the diaspora, which is read and reconfigured by and in urban India and the diaspora, which returns to reshape Bollywood cinema itself. Exemplary star figures such as Shahrukh Khan emerge in the assemblage of Hindi cinema that offer a desire about, and mediate, the homeland and the diaspora through their on- and off-screen performances, using their body in literal and metaphoric ways to enunciate particular kinds of social and economic aspirations. Through the use of cinematic technology these aspirations are given the illusion of reality that can be further arbitrated by audiences as partial scripts in the formation of their social selves.

The notion of the cinematic assemblage as a conceptual framework to consider the production of and workings of desire, representation and circuits of cultural globalisation amidst the flows of technology, social affect and actual cultural geographies has been used throughout this book. At times the assemblage of Bollywood has been touched upon and alluded to in the analyses of each chapter and at other times rendered explicit, as in Chapter 4. What the analysis of the cinematic assemblages of the two cinema houses in New York (the Eagle in Jackson Heights and the Loews in Times

Square) reveals is the further need to map out and account for the actualisation of desire in the workings of Bollywood cinema. Specifically, in the act of Bollywood cinema going in the South Asian diasporas of the West, the textual representations of Bollywood films as part scripts of local and global affects and as articulated with media technology and aspirational commodity cultures have been illustrated in the development of Bollywood cinema in the contemporary moment.

In Chapters 2 and 3 Bollywood cinema has been shown to be in the midst of a culturally hegemonic struggle in which its middle-class Hindu constituency is often hailed as an imagined community in the urban centres of India and also through the representation of the diaspora. However, that middle-class identity is often contested through the representation of other social groups and also contested further by readings of the films by audiences in the wider South Asian diaspora. One important constituent of the audiences as social actors in the diaspora is the queer audience as shown in Chapter 5. These audiences not only reread the conservative and patriarchal boy-meets-girl love stories in the films, moreover they redeploy the Bollywood song and dance sequences in the urban diasporic space of the queer club night and transform them into new cultural translations and possibilities that are part of a cultural politics that interrogate the relationship between the homeland and the diaspora in which gender and sexual difference is often subsumed under a socially constructed heteronormativity. Subsequently, contemporary Bollywood cinema has begun to increasingly include queer representations and aesthetics in its films. In this way South Asians are not just simple audiences of and for Bollywood media texts, but by using these texts in the daily and partial formation of their lives they are social actors too. Chapter 5 has also highlighted that a much longer and ambivalent queer history exists in the formation of the popular Hindi cinematic apparatus that begs further consideration and exploration.

Chapter 6 situates Bollywood cinema within the context of globalisation both textually in terms of the changes taking place in the aesthetics of the films themselves as sources of cultural mimicry, and in operational terms through the increasing co-production possibilities that are taking shape between different players in its local and global industry. The workings of Bollywood amidst globalisation creates a number of possibilities ranging from the innovative adaptation, through to the 'cut and pasting' of ideas, from different cinematic sources which audiences are quick to identify and enjoy— or to criticise as unoriginal—and also for the genuine collaboration of film co-production in terms of finance and content development. Attention has also been paid to the utilisation of Bollywood aesthetics in episodes from select films from diasporic South Asian film-makers to consider the social and aesthetic effects of and changes to Bollywood cinema as it is taken up to articulate some of the cultural politics and social concerns of these films. Both sociologically and aesthetically these films, as examples of global cultural production, create a fluid cinematic language that takes us between and beyond the cinemas of Hollywood and Bollywood.

The preceding chapters have thus set into play a dialogue between sociology and studies of the cinema. Whilst acknowledging the sometimes shifting tone, pace and cross-disciplinary emphasis of this dialogue, we are now able to contemplate further what happens to the analysis of Bollywood cinema through sociological enquiry? And what happens to sociology when it considers a complex social, cultural and media phenomenon such as Bollywood cinema?

In terms of a response to the first question, this is best posed by recalling the critical synergies and insights available to us through an alliance of the work of Norman Denzin on cinema and the collective and numerous works of scholars of popular Hindi cinema that have been put forward in Chapter 1. Taken together, this body of work fosters a sociological imagination—i.e., a critical examination of the private and public dimensions of cinema and society, and how we might best begin to interpret their interrelationships—that is put it to use through part social insight and commentary (theoretical frameworks), part close textual-based readings (aesthetic analyses), and part qualitative immersion (methodologically). In this way it is possible to formulate a theory of Bollywood cinema that is able to locate it within a social matrix that does not lose sight of the people at the heart of its intended and unpredictable cultural emissions— its audiences as social actors. This, then, becomes a theory of Bollywood cinema that does not shy away from its representations (of for example caste, class, gender and sexuality, religion, communal politics, nation, diaspora and globalisation) and their possible power and violence. Instead it is also a theory that intervenes in and demonstrates the ability of film-makers and audiences as engaging in these instances through complex ways in the workings of the

cinematic assemblage/apparatus as industry, rather than through
interpretations that fix their meaning in advance through limiting
predetermined analyses at best, and dismissive populist criticisms at
worse.

In response to the second question, just as the cultural and social
have been placed at the heart of the understandings of Bollywood
cinema, then we must also reemphasise the possibility of the subject
of sociology as playing an important role in making sense of those
dimensions, particularly in conjunction with different subject areas
with related areas of interest. In particular, sociology has been
presented throughout this book through the sociological imagination
which implies a critical interrogation of the taken-for-granted assumptions about modern cultural and social spheres of aspects of
Indian and diasporic South Asian life as they are given expression
through, and themselves express relationships with, the cinematic
idioms and popular cultures of Bollywood. Operationally, this involves a combined textual outline, aesthetic analyses framed within
select, yet flexible methodologies, and a simultaneous socio-cultural
critique of the personal and collective possibilities engendered through
the popular Hindi cinema from Mumbai. In this way the sociological
imagination encourages us with a way of wanting to know, of wanting
to engage with the popular cultures of cinema through a 'multi-
sensual, multi-perspectival epistemology that does not privilege sight
(vision) over the other senses, including sound, touch and taste'
(Denzin 1995: 218). This imagination becomes a way of wanting to
know cinema and its related popular cultures through not just an
anlysis of representation alone, but by interrogating the structures,
the actual formation and workings of the apparatus of cinema as
it works and is reworked through local and global nodes and circuits.
The imagination applied to cinema, then, is a creative one that places
emphasis on the part of the viewer, the spectator, the audience, the
reader, to consider his/her investments in the construction of knowledge about meaning-making in, and from the contexts of, cinema:
a cinema where desire is created and recreated as it is criss-crossed
by dimensions of socio-cultural power relations and where the
sensations of the body are mediated and actualised through affect
as Bollywood continues to become global, commodified and capitalist; yet without its end pre-determined for any given length or in
any fixed way. It becomes imperative, therefore, for a sociological
imagination applied to cinema to extend and multiply its frames of

reference in order to be able to speculate further the possibilities that have been put forward in this book.

Extending the insights of Chapter 3, for instance, where actor Shahrukh Khan was introduced as the current favoured urban Indian and diasporic male character and star, is it possible to consider equally fascinating heroines for comparison? Two contemporary leading star actresses are of note here: Aishwarya Rai and Rani Mukherjee. Both have successfully mediated rural and urban Indian and diasporic assemblages in their performances as actresses and through the use of their star bodies in recent films. Rai for example in *Hum Dil De Chuke Sanam* (1999), *Devdas* (2002) and *Bride and Prejudice* (2004) and Mukherjee in *Kuch Kuch Hota Hai* (1998), *Saathiya* (2002) and *Bunty Aur Babli* (2005), to name a few of their relevant films. Both actresses are also important players in terms of using their star personas to endorse national and international global consumer brands and desires. Rai endorses the expensive Longines watches within India and abroad, and Mukherjee endorses Coca-Cola India's orange drink Fanta in the north of the country. Furthermore, Rai has been accredited as making a noticeable crossover into Hollywood and British cinemas with the realease of *Bride and Prejudice* and her anticipated forthcoming film *The Mistress of Spices*, based on the bestselling novel by Chitra Divakaruni. These brief bios of our two current leading star actresses sets up a wider context in which to consider how they might allow a consideration of gendered female rural and urban Indian and diasporic-homeland mediations and possibilities through their starring roles and personal and professional lives.

In order to pursue further a multi-sensual perspective on cinema that allows us to extrapolate qualitative cultural and social insights from its study, we might do well to elaborate and make haptic a sociological imagination as applied to cinema. This would entail accounting for the ways in which the touch of sight also responds to, and with, the touch of other senses—the vibrations of sound and their potential to affect desires and emotions would be a case in point. Applied to popular Hindi cinema this would allow us to examine further the ways in which film songs have been argued through as part of a hegemonic cultural contestation, as in Chapter 2, and also pursued in terms of the ways in which songs, music and dance—as they literally vibrate and make sound and body come to life through cinema's technological apparatus—are also crucial to the assemblage of Bollywood in which desire can be situated and made sense of similarly and differentially in specific cultural spaces (cf. Chapter 4). In this way, the analytical frameworks of 'cultural hegemony' and 'the production of desire' are at once implicated in a relationship of social formation and power that can be potentially contested and reframed.

A focus on queer *desis* in Chapter 5 lends itself to be developed as a queer sociological imagination that renders visible the placing of minority or marginal alterities in relation to each other—for example, race, ethnicity, gender and sexuality. This becomes a call for uncovering the intersection of cultural differences as a starting point for the hybrid and 'culturally impure' to continue their projects of social formation with a potential to, at the very least, disrupt existing heteronormative ways that can exert oppression through their own cultural and social spheres of organisation. A continued focus on the possibilities arising out of Bollywood cinema and its popular cultures that might be useful in such formations, beyond the limits of the argument put forward here, necessitates this project further.

If in Chapter 6 paying attention to the local and global nexus of contemporary Bollywood production and distribution has allowed us to read some of the social possibilities and fluid cinematic aesthetics that are created between and beyond Bollywood cinemas, then this also provides us with cues and insights for a mindful imagination; one that is able to observe the development of co-production possibilities (say between India and the US, or between India and Pakistan) and their continued fluidity, or not as the case maybe, in terms of globalised cultural production.

Ultimately, then, the multifaceted nature of the workings of Bollywood cinema—from industry, to audiences, to its wider popular culture—necessitates an elaboration of the medium through various and simultaneous modes of enquiry. The mode of enquiry of sociology that enables us to qualitatively interpret aspects of culture and society, while reading and engaging with cinema and its popular cultures, can further benefit from being amplified, filtered, refracted, co-edited and refocused as it goes to the movies.

Appendix
Six Genres of
Bollywood Films

The six genres of Bollywood films can be characterised as follows:

Devotional Films

Devotional films, sometimes referred to as mythologicals, are the films with which the Indian film industry started and their influence continues to the present day. Religious in tone, these were the first films made by the industry and they helped revive national traditions under threat from British imperial rule. The first feature film, made in 1913, *Raja Harischandra* (dir. H. Phalke) was a Hindu mythological. With Hinduism dating back some 5,000 years the majority of devotional films are based upon Hindu myths and legends of the gods and demi-gods and their adventures on earth. Other films are based on the lives of religious men and women. The watching of these films is often considered a religious experience in itself by many audiences. The influence of devotionals can be found in all types of Indian cinema: constant reference to God, to fate, past lives and future births that is present even in the most modern thriller. Islamic, Christian and Sikh devotional films have been made and people of different faiths often appreciate the same film. However, these films as a popular mass medium were also the early purveyors of a high Brahmanical caste and middle-class status-quo (see Rai 1994: 58–60).

HISTORICAL FILMS

After the advent of sound in Indian cinema (1931) historical films came to the fore. These films told elaborate stories based upon real characters from Indian history and associated legendary tales. Historicals further progressed the awakening national consciousness of India throughout the thirties. Whilst harking back to the glories of the past, subtle references would remind the audience of present foreign domination. Some were overtly political in character and were banned by the British but sometimes secret screenings were arranged in resistance and defiance (see Rai 1994: 53–62 for a critical and historical overview of pre-Independence Indian cinema). Edward Johnson describes these films as displaying '[t]he splendour of pre-Raj India, the costumes, nobility and drama were presented with an emotional thrust that did much to re-establish Indian national esteem' (1987: 2). *Mughal-E-Azam* (dir. K. Asif, 1960), although made after Independence, is perhaps the best known of this genre of films. It opens with a voice-over which says 'I am Hindustan' spoken over a map of India and then, in flashback, goes onto to tell the ill-fated, yet daring love story of the Mughal Prince Salim (Dilip Kumar) and slave girl Anarkali (Madhubala). Away from the direct tyranny of the British Empire post-Independence historicals reworked what had become distorted accounts of India's struggle for freedom. For example, a number of films re-enacted the Indian Mutiny thereby lending a fascinating Indian perspective on an event that has been much worked upon in neo-colonial terms in the Western mass media. As a case in point, *Jhansi Ki Rani* (Queen of Jhansi), made in 1953 and directed by Sorab Modi, spectacularly chronicles the life of Queen Lakshmibai (Mehtab) of Jhansi who led her armies into battle against the British East India Company during the 1857 uprising.

SOCIAL FILMS (SOMETIMES CALLED TOPICALS)

Socials films comprised the largest group of films between India's immediate years of Independence and transition 1947–60. As India moved towards independence, the past was subterfuged and more contemporary themes were addressed in its cinema. Social films cover similar ground to Western, fifties melodramas, film noir or post-war neo-realist films. Invoking emotion and social consciousness in their audiences social films address themselves to the changes taking place in culture and society, including the complex interplay of personal identity, love, human relationships, family and the law. *Devdas* (dir. Bimal Roy, 1955) dealt with the tragic consequences of enforced arranged marriages and the caste system. *Ganga Jumna* (dir. Nitin Bhose, 1961) reveals the inadequacies of a corrupt and emotionless legal system that posits a wrongly accused Ganga (Dilip Kumar) against his righteous police brother Jumna (N. Kumar). More recent social films have explored the secondary role of women in Indian society and their exploitation by men. Evidently, this challenges the notion that Indian cinema is simply escapist as, in the words of Edward Johnson, '[t]he emotional reaction of the audience to the film is based very much in reality and a knowledge of the real experiences and dilemmas explored in the film' (Johnson 1987: 3).

The importance given to passion or emotion in these films perhaps attracts criticism that these films contain ridiculous stories, absurd coincidence and/or hysterical acting. Yet the same criticisms could be labelled at most operas, much of Shakespeare and Dickens' stories of Victorian life. Production values are concentrated especially in song picturisation in which the inner conflicts, thoughts and feelings of the protagonists are explored. It is in this genre that some of India's greatest directors have worked: Bimal Roy, Guru Dutt and Mehboob.

MUSLIM SOCIAL FILMS

This genre is perhaps best understood as a sub-category of the socials. Muslim socials were especially popular in the sixties. Their appeal is far wider than the 10 per cent Muslim composition of India and reflects the immense Islamic heritage in the country and also in the film industry where a disproportionate number of actors, writers and musicians are Muslim. Interestingly, the Bollywood film industry was the first place in modern India where all caste and sect barriers were broken down and to this day the film community is popularly known as one of the most progressive 'multicultural' forces in the subcontinent promoting inter-religious and inter-ethnic harmony. Part of the appeal of Muslim socials is the vast opportunity given by them to music, poetry and dance. The stories are often inspired by Urdu love poetry: the impossibility of true love, love across social divides, love at first sight, love equated with divinity, love triangles and so forth. Visually, the films delight in recreating a world of urban pleasure or courtly upper-class opulence. *Umrao Jaan* (dir. Muzzafar Ali, 1980), starring the actress Rekha who plays a courtesan dancer caught between the ills of her profession and the love for a landed nobleman played by Faroque Sheikh, is perhaps one of the better known examples of this genre of films.

MASALA FILMS

The masala or all-action films are often the ones mistaken to represent all Bollywood films as formulaic or 'the same' in the uncritical imagination. Johnson reveals that this type of film was actually anticipated in the late sixties by a type of 'B' movie called stunt films which were rather like the American Zorro or Marvelman serials (Johnson 1987: 2). Masala films are loaded with glamour and have been popular with the urban working class. They represent the hopes and anxieties of the everyman in a fast-changing world. The angry young man series of films of the seventies starring Amitabh Bachchan, such as *Deewaar* (dir. Yash Chopra, 1975) and *Muqaddar Ka Sikandar* (dir. Prakash Mehra, 1978), are good examples of the masala genre. Masala films draw upon all aspects of Indian popular culture for their formulae. In a loosely knit story one can see big city underworld crime, martial arts fights scenes with exaggerated hitting noises—'dishum, dishum'—car stunts, sexy cabarets, elaborate dance sequences, comedy, romance and family melodrama. The appeal of these films is spectacle and emotion and everything is designed to give maximum impact. Johnson (ibid.: 4) likens the appeal of this genre of movies to that of James Bond films for Western audiences. The producers are challenged by the audience to continually think up something more spectacular, more imaginative, more bizarre with which to assault the senses. At their worst masala films are kitsch rubbish but at their best they are enthralling entertainment and have audiences reeling with laughter and tears from one minute to the next.

During the nineties, all-action films suffered a blow in terms of the decline in audience attendance and takings at the box-office in

India. As a case in point, *Salaakhen* (Barrier, dir. Guddu Dhanoa, 1998) was produced at a cost of Rs 8 million but made a loss of Rs 3.5 million. *Kabhi na Kabhi* (Sooner or Later, dir. Priyadarshan, 1998) was made at Rs 5.5 million but made a staggering loss of Rs 4 million (see Chopra 1998: 46–47). For decades the masala movie was thought to be a guaranteed success to recover production costs and boost profits. This is no longer the case as when romantic films like *Hum Aapke Hain Koun..!* (Who am i to you) and *Dilwale Dulhaniya Le Jayenge* (The Braveheart Will Take the Bride) released in the mid-nineties, they inspired a feel-good factor which brought back urban cinema audiences in India and across the diaspora in large numbers after the slump in attendance figures caused by competition from video and non-terrestrial media. Audiences also began to slacken away from the tried and tested formulas of the masala films. The period of the late nineties, then, saw film teams associated with all-action films as redirecting their energies and finances towards more rounded family entertainers, consisting of a more palatable blend of romance and peppered with action only when required according to the script. Male stars like Akshay Kumar, Sunil Shetty and Sunny Deol have also undergone a transformation in recent years from their young, hard men screen personas to believable heroes with more credible causes to defend.

THE ROMANTIC GENRE

This genre of films is dominating the current success at the box-office both in India and throughout the South Asian diaspora. Almost all the big Bollywood earners of the past few years have been romantic films. *Pardes*, the film discussed in Chapter 3, falls under this category. Romance and eroticism have always featured highly across the spectrum of Indian cinema and romantic films have been popular from the very beginning of Bollywood movies in particular. Overt sexuality is prohibited in Indian films, thus much is conveyed through suggestion, innuendo, coded signs and symbols. Songs and dances play a crucial role wherein eroticism and sexuality are often closely linked with song and dance numbers (Kasbekar 1996: 369–70). Gokulsing and Dissanayake (1998) observe that in order to better appreciate the meanings of romantic films we need to reconnect them with wider South Asian historical traditions of love stories from which these films emanate. In this regard, the Laila-Majnu (two Muslim lovers from the period of pre-Mughal India) and Radha-Krishna (Gods from the Hindu faith) traditions are important:

> In the Laila Majnu tradition, love is seen as the essential desire of God; earthly love is regarded as a preparation for heavenly love. The absolute devotion of the woman to the man, marital fidelity, loving secretly but without guilt are important aspects of this tradition. The Radha Krishna tradition, on the other hand, emphasises the here and the now, the desire to capture the joy of each moment as it passes. Love is seen not as tragic but as tender and joyous (Gokulsing and Dissanayake 1998: 26).

In a broad sense, then, six distinct genres of Bollywood films can be detected. A seventh genre of films can also be seen to exist that of the contemporary horror or supernatural films that have included, of late, *Bhoot* (Ghost, dir. Ram Gopal Verma, 2003) or *Kaal* (Time to Die, dir. Soham Shah, 2005). However, these must not be consigned as rigid generic definitions as Bollywood films often display layers of inter-textuality and cross-fertilisations of different genres within films. For example, it wouldn't be odd for a masala film to consist of elements of any or all of the six genres mentioned here, or for a social film to relay its social message more effectively by way of a song and dance sequence inspired by the muslim social films. It is important to be aware of, and make critical readings of, the cultural inscriptions that loosely comprise each genre of Bollywood films. It is these cultural inscriptions that give Bollywood cinema its distinctive appeal and attachment with audiences.

NOTES

INTRODUCTION

1. Rupak Mann was often referred to—by herself, the wider British media who took an interest in the programme, other finalists, and viewers of the programme—as 'the fat woman of the show'. Rupak Mann subverted any negative connotations around her obese weight by often using phrases like 'it's not over until the fat lady sings' and went on to win a role in a Bollywood film. The underdog winning in *Bollywood Star* was surprisingly in keeping with Bollywood cinema's often championing of the underdog as a character or thematic representation in many of its films.
2. On the emergence of the Zee TV channel in Europe, see Dudrah (2005).

CHAPTER 1: TOWARDS A SOCIOLOGY OF CINEMA

1. On this history and the kinds of studies that emerged see Turner (1998). See also the introduction and chapters in Tinkcom and Villarejo (2001) for more recent cultural and sociological explorations of film.
2. I will not enter here, in this chapter, into an exhaustive list or summary of the main findings, important contributions or otherwise of each of these authors. Their arguments, where relevant and appropriate, are taken up for further analysis and critique throughout the book in each of the chapters that follow.
3. Interestingly, the post-1947 independent period of popular Indian cinema has received most attention and the pre-independent cinema still requires

much research (on early cinema see, for example, Bandyopadhyay 1993; Barnouw and Krishnaswamy 1980; Garga 1996; Kaul 1998; Rajadhyaksha and Willemen 1994).

4. In this view, the Bollywood film is considered as 'a cultural product that has been historically circumscribed by the psychodynamics of orality—that is, by the thought processes and personality structures that distinguish a non-writing mindset, and, as such, it is a product that employs specific devices and motifs that are traditionally part of orally based storytelling' (Nayar 2004: 14).

5. See www.bollywoodshows.com for more. Date last accessed: 17 December 2004.

6. The Telugu film industry has been popularly referred to as 'Tollywood'. Interestingly, the capital of the Pakistani film industry based in Lahore has been popularly referred to as 'Lollywood'. See Mushtaq Gazdar (1997) for an account of Pakistani cinema as emerging and developing from the Indian subcontinent's cinemas during the pre- and post-Partition years.

7. More recent reports suggest that the annual cinema attendance figure is approximately around 6 billion visits (see Power and Mazumdar 2000).

8. Contributors to Murphy (2000) cite a maximum high of 114 million visits to UK cinemas in 1979.

9. For example, the economics and the role of the Indian state in Bollywood film production remains to be fully charted. Ashok Mital in his *Cinema Industry in India* (1995), focusing primarily on the pricing and taxation of films, notes that the 'economics of entertainment is a highly under-researched area of study' and that literature on this subject is 'scant and academic works are far and few between'. Thus, definitions and working descriptions of what constitutes 'economics' in Bollywood film production remain to be outlined and elaborated in order to understand the relationships between the inception of the idea of a film, through to its funding, filming, post-production, distribution and exhibition. This might well include an understanding of the role of producers, sources of finance and distributors, the popularity and sale of film music albums, and how the workings of these interrelated processes might help explain the cultural impact and success, or not, of particular movies. More recently, Tejaswini Ganti (2004: 53–56) describes the workings of the Hindi film industry as decentralised and fragmented in terms of its production, distribution and exhibition when compared to the Hollywood film industry.

For an outline of the process involved in making Bollywood movies, see Gokulsing and Dissanayake (1998: 102), and on the breakdown of estimated costs for producing a popular Hindi film, see Ganti (2004: 57).

10. By drawing on the methods of qualitative interviews and participant observation an attempt has been made to elaborate on and give a textured feeling to the films and their related popular cultures that are taken up for analysis and comment in this book.

11. Mishra usefully differentiates the different strands of Indian mass migration and their ensuing diasporas. The first wave of Indian displacement occurred during colonialism comprising of indentured labourers to service the British plantation economy. These populations he classifies as the diaspora of classic capitalism. The second major migration of Indians occurred after the sixties and is a response to the pressures of post-war social and urban

restructuring and late capitalism, and was directed primarily at the metropolitan centres of the West.

12. Mishra's study, apart from the use of Gillespie, remains an exciting and
illuminating account of the aspects of Bollywood cinema. Gillespie's work
has been critiqued by some for applying the anthropological gaze at South
Asians as 'others', albeit in an ethnically sensitised manner. For useful
reviews and critiques of Gillespie's work, see Hutnyk (1996), Sharma (1996:
34–35) and Raj (1998).

13. In this context, global cultural commodity markets are understood as operating for the exchange of cultural goods and texts, such as films, for
maximum profit and also to enhance the international esteem of the products being sold.

CHAPTER 2: SINGING FOR INDIA: SONGS IN THE BOLLYWOOD FILM

1. Quoted in Jeremy Marre and Hannah Charlton (1985: 138). The term
'Music Director' is the commonly used term in Bollywood for the role which
would equate with Music Composer in Western cinema, although the role
of Music Director is more central to Bollywood films, as is explained in the
chapter.

2. Jane Feuer's book is an often-cited work on Hollywood musicals that makes
it an interesting point of contrast to consider the workings of song and music
in Bollywood cinema in this chapter.

3. For example, regional folk theatres, and classical dancing such as the
mudras, discussed in the reading of *Hum Aapke Hain Koun..!*

4. Although this is a heterosexual paradigm, there is a tradition of sexual
difference to the heterosexual norm deeply rooted within Indian culture,
such as the hijra way of life, transvestites and homosexuality. See Chapter 5 on queer and camp South Asian audiences reworking and re-reading
Bollywood songs and dance in the urban diasporic gay and lesbian club.

5. See the 'Mythologicals' entry in Ashish Rajadhyaksha and Paul Willemen
(1994: 145); and in the Appendix to this book.

6. An early film, *Indrasabha* (1925), quoted in Asha Kasbekar (1996: 369).

7. This is particularly true of the dismissive and populist Western commentaries
often levelled at Bollywood cinema in the Western mass media, some
examples of which are highlighted in Chapter 6 (for example, Malcolm
1989).

8. Sandeep Unnithan (2004).

9. This was even more so in the days before audio cassettes, when record
players and vinyl were beyond financial reach for the majority of Indians.
See Manuel 1993: 60.

10. See the 'All-India Film' entry in Rajadhyaksha and Willemen (1994: 41).

11. Hereafter cited as *HAHK*.

12. *Movie International*, March 1995: 23.

13. See Chaudhary 1998; Goldenberg and Dodd 1998; Joshi 1998 and Tyrrell
1998.

14   See for instance Nikhat Kazmi (1998: 186–92).
15. On the more pernicious aspects of how Bollywood cinema has been appro-
     priated by right-wing Hindutva politics in India, see Kazmi (1999: 12–15)
     and Mishra (2002: Chapter 7).
16. See, for instancem, Vamsee K. Juluri (1999) and Patricia Uberoi (2001) on
     audience readings of *HAHK* in Hyderabad and in Delhi, India, respectively.
17. This same trio, with the stars of the film (Salman Khan and Madhuri Dixit),
     helped produce the film's most popular song, 'Didi tera devar deewaana'
     (Sister your brother-in-law is mad). This song not only became a sensation
     through all of India, but even to this day is quoted and translated in
     contemporary Bollywood movies.
18. Copies of Madhuri Dixit's costumes in the film were much sought after in
     India and across the diaspora after the film's release.
19. The two films *Fiza* and *Chalte Chalte* are indicative of longer trajectories
     of representation in the history of popular Hindi cinema—i.e., part of the
     genres of Muslim social films, and the modern-day urban romance respec-
     tively.
20. It is interesting to note that when the BBC broadcasted a short season of
     Bollywood movies on weekend mornings they cut the songs to save time,
     thereby fundamentally missing the point. For example, UK terrestrial broad-
     caster BBC2's screening of *Chachi 420* (Aunty 420, dir. Kamal Hassan,
     1998) in January 2000 cut every song from the movie.

CHAPTER 3: READING POPULAR HINDI FILMS IN THE DIASPORA AND THE PERFORMANCE OF URBAN INDIAN AND DIASPORIC IDENTITY

1.   The empirical data used in this chapter is based on research undertaken
     for my doctoral study on the use of diasporic music, film and non-terrestrial
     television in the city of Birmingham, UK, by young British Asians (see
     Dudrah 2001). A total of 23 extended interviews were conducted with 14–
     26-year-old British South Asians for this work. Interviews were conducted
     after the use of an initial questionnaire survey that was used in a conscious
     attempt to identify respondents who wished to be interviewed further.
     Methods such as qualitative extended interviews proved useful in this re-
     search where meanings of popular cultures were sought amongst young
     British Asians. The interview extracts used in this chapter were conducted
     during December 1997 and February 1998. The nine respondents quoted
     here, who appear under pseudonyms of their own choice, are as following:

     Reshmo: 17- year-old female, A-level student.
     Babs: 17-year-old female, A-level student.
     Madhuri: 21-year-old female, undergraduate degree student.
     Nahid: 21-year-old female, undergraduate degree student.
     Bally: 26-year-old female, insurance clerk.
     Taran: 18-year-old female, A-level student.

Kully: 20-year-old male, A-level student.

Rita: 24-year-old female, crime bureau officer.

Manjit: 22-year-old male, bank clerk.

2. Ganti describes the five major territories as: Bombay (Mumbai), Delhi/Uttar Pradesh/East Punjab, Central Province/Central India/Rajasthan, Eastern and South. These five territories can be divided further into 14 sub-territories. The sixth major overseas territory is subdivided into North America, United Kingdom, Gulf States, South Africa, etc.

3. This film has gone on to become the longest running film still showing in Indian cinemas in Mumbai—in June 2005 it has entered its 500th successful week of cinema exhibition—and is also one of the all-time favourites of contemporary Bollywood cinema amongst diasporic Indians.

4. See film review of *Pardes* by Mohammad Ali Ikram at http://planetbollywood.com/Film/pardes1.html and Vishal Ghadia at http://in.rediff.com/movies/2003/oct/23pardes.htm, both sites accessed on 22 June 2004.

5. I concur here with Virdi's (2003: 197) reading of Mankekar's essay.

6. It is not being argued here that in Goffman's work there exists an implied simple 'real self', rather it is suggested that a combination between Goffman's work and work in Drama and Theatre Studies is a useful way to begin to consider the possible relationships between identity and performance.

7. The film's end credits cite Mr Chanchai Inthasan and Mr Kecha Kumpukdee as doubling for Shahrukh Khan and Sunil Shetty respectively.

8. see http://www.bollywoodmantra.com/website/article413.html, last accessed on 9 August 2004.

CHAPTER 4: BOLLYWOOD CINEMA GOING IN NEW YORK

1. Participant observation was undertaken simultaneously at these two sites by myself and my co-researcher Dr Amit Rai, Florida State University, USA. The observations presented in this chapter are part of a wider piece of research that was granted an award by the British Academy's Joint International Activities Scheme examining Bollywood cinema going in Manchester (UK) and in New York City. The collective terms 'our' and 'we' mentioned throughout the chapter refers to the dialogue and conversations between, and fieldwork carried out by, Amit and myself. The research involved participant observation and informal conversations with cinema audiences at the Eagle and Loews theatres in New York, as well as further semi-structured interviews with 15 American South Asians. Although these latter qualitative interviews are not used in this chapter in a fuller sense, they are referred to where they help to elaborate on some of the points being made.

2. Jackson Heights and the borough of Queens has been a highly racially profiled area by the US authorities since 9/11 due to the large number of South Asians living there. Racial attacks (hate crimes) against South Asians throughout the States have also been on the rise, including a violent physical

attack on a South Asian Sikh family in Jackson Heights in August 2003. See Shams Tarek and Azi Paybarah, 'A Community Unites After Bias Attack', *Queens Tribune*, 11 August 2003, reproduced at http://www.nynice.org/Tribune%20August_11_03_.htm, last accessed on 1 October 2004.

3. John Roleke, 'A Tour of Jackson Heights, A South Asian Neighborhood', http://queens.about.com/cs/neighborhoods/a/jackson_heights.htm, last accessed on May 2004.

4. For instance the 1998 film *Aa Ab Laut Chalen* (Come Let Us Return, dir. Rishi Kapoor) is set in Jackson Heights and considers the travails of Indian immigrant location to the US.

5. For the marketing of Jackson Heights for tourists in New York City see http://newyork.citysearch.com/feature/37418/sande.html, last accessed on August 2003.

6. The term '*desi*' is used by diasporic South Asians from the South Asian vernacular to refer to themselves as having a socio-cultural attachment to their respective homelands.

7. Wade Nacinovich, 'The Eagle Theatre: Bollywood in Jackson Heights', http://members.cox.net/casajp2/maitra/bollywood.html, last accessed on August 2003.

8. H1-B Visas are used to bring a non-immigrant worker to the US if the employee is able to fill a position in a specialty occupation for professional position. The employee must prove that he/she is qualified for the position, holding a foreign degree equivalent to that required in the US. The visa can be granted from one to six years after which time he/she must reside outside the US for at least one year. See http://www.computeruser.com/resources/dictionary/definition.html?lookup=8221, last accessed on August 2004.

9. Smith 2003.

10. My colleague Amit Rai and I have together delivered versions of this research in three separate locations in Europe—Frankfurt, Manchester and London. In each context, we have been taken to task for dabbling in rasa theory. At its most inane, the argument against engaging with rasa (as one of the material conditions of the media-body assemblage in the globalising contexts of contemporary Bollywood) devolves into an objection that its use invites a Hindu nationalist reading. Nothing could be further from its effects. Bringing a consideration of rasa into a conversation on how the body is being reconstituted through this assemblage—how, in effect, new habituations are created through the articulation of bodily sensations, affects, diegetic and actual local–global desires through the Bollywood cinematic assemblage—makes rasa, such a conversation, the strategic flux of bodily juices, and its use seems highly appropriate to initiate this dialogue here.

11. On rasa theory, see Bimal Mukherjee and Sunil Kothari 1995; Priyadarshi Patnaik 1997; David Waterhouse 1998; Suvarnalata Rao 2000 and Vijay Mishra 2002.

12. Note, also, that the first play performed by Bharata—composed by Brahma (one the most revered of the gods) and performed at his request—is a 'Samavakara' called 'Amrta-Manthana' which is supposed to enlighten the audience—'about duty (*dharma*), prosperity (*artha* = earning wealth) and desire (*kama* = the inner urge in man)', Rangacharya (1996: 22).

13. Adya Rangacharya, 'About the Natyasastra', in *The Natyasastra*, translated by Adya Rangacharya (New Delhi: Munshiram Manoharlal, 1996), p. xxii.

14. On the use of participant observation as a method for cultural and social research with media audiences see, for example, Jensen 2002 and Schroder et al. 2003.

15. See Lalitha Gopalan (2002). Gopalan refers to song and dance sequences, the interval, and aesthetic responses to state censorship as different kinds of interruptions in the narratives of popular Indian cinema that enable a commentary on the relationship between the spectator/audience and the nation state as one produced in the complex local and global circulation of Hindi cinema.

16. For example, following the logic of supplementarity famously noted by Derrida (1983), the director is always supplemented by a host of others—producer, star persona, choreographer, art director and music director, to name only five.

17. Hrithik Roshan's father launched his son's film career in *Kaho Na... Pyar Hai* (Say That There is Love, 2000) that went on to be a hit film at the box office, instantly propelling Hrithik Roshan to stardom. *Koi... Mil Gaya* was the second film outing between father and son after three years. In between, Hrithik Roshan had a roller coaster ride of box-office flops with his other films. Thus, the pairing of father and son again was much anticipated by audiences as well the Bollywood film industry. *Koi... Mil Gaya* went on to do well at the box office and was widely received with good reviews by audiences and critics alike, especially for Hrithik's role as a mentally-challenged adult. At both Eagle and Loews, while audiences vacated the cinema hall, we overheard several spectators commenting on how well Hrithik had acted.

18. The need to observe and comment on the similarities and differences between haptic spaces is being argued for here. In fact, such overlaps and dissonances have to be placed alongside one another in order to further map out the possibilities inherent in the filmic text(s) as they are articulated in such differing and related haptic spaces of reception.

19. This was illustrated even further when during our research in August, New York, amongst other cities on America's north-eastern coast, experienced a major electronic power shortage that was referred to as a 'blackout' (14 August 2003). Amidst fears of another 9/11-style attack, one of the first places that was switched on when energy was restored some several hours later, was Times Square. Ironically, this was amidst official calls throughout the media for New Yorkers to conserve energy in their homes by only switching on the domestic appliances they crucially required.

20. This strange alliance of the state and ideological forms of services and entertainment by and for the privileged classes can be seen in the presentation of the New York Police Department's public booth in Times Square which is lit-up in bright purple and pink fluorescent neon lights.

21. For an overview of how this mid-nineties municipal anxiety to control and Disney-fy Times Square is part of a much longer history about the clearing of the area of prostitutes, sex shops and crime since the turn of the twentieth century, see http://www.timessquare.com/history/history_101.html, http://www.timessquare.com/history/sex_and_the_square.html, and http://hellskitchen.net/issues/tsbidsex/history.html, all accessed last on March 2004.

22. See Daniel Smith 2003: 32.

23. For short- and long-term memory, see Deleuze and Guattari 1983: 34.

Chapter 5: Queer as *Desis*: Secret Politics of Gender and Sexuality in Bollywood Films in Diasporic Urban Ethnoscapes

1. See for instance *Life The Observer Magazine*, 7 April 2002, London.
2. Bollywood as a source of entertainment was signalled as 'other', a recurrent feature of orientalism (Said 1978), and as from a faraway place, India and the East more generally, that was made available in the UK thereby playing up to notions of exotica in the contemporary present.
3. For an example of such film criticism see David Cook 1996: 861.
4. Throughout this chapter, 'queer' is used as an umbrella term exploring the social construction and performance of different gender and sexual identities such as gay, lesbian, bisexual and heterosexual. It also involves a critique and displacement of heteronormative structures and predominantly straight desires.
   The term camp refers to the in-betweeness and slippages in the performance of gender and sexual identities, drawing attention to the ambivalences and problematics in the performance of gender and sexual identities as not quite coherent or whole.
5. I am less interested in nostalgic understandings of and attachments to the homeland through Bollywood cinema and am more interested in exploring the possibilities for new social and cultural formations that render problematic any simple formulations of the homeland and its diaspora. This encourages us to make a point of departure, a new line of flight as it were.
6. See the Birmingham South Asian gay and lesbian club night's website at www.saathinight.com, date accessed 25 February 2004. See the Leicester South Asian gay and lesbian club night's website at www.clubishq.com, date accessed 25 February 2004. See the London South Asian gay and lesbian club night's website at www.clubkali.co.uk, date accessed 25 February 2004. See the Manchester South Asian gay and lesbian club night's website at www.clubzindagi.com, date accessed 25 February 2004.
7. See New York City (NYC) South Asian gay and lesbian club night's website at www.sholayevents.com, date accessed 25 February 2004. Of note here is the work of Sunaina Maira (2002) on South Asian American youth club culture in NYC. Although she acknowledges, in passing, the existence of separate queer *desi* club nights and also the existence of queer *desis* at predominantly heterosexual club events in NYC, she concurs that queer *desi* parties in North America exist as parallel to 'often aggressively heterosexual bhangra remix youth subculture where queerness was invisible' (Maira 2002: 47–48).
8. See, for example, the collection of essays on Asian American sexualities that discuss, amongst other things, the formation of Asian queer identities in relation to white racism in its heteronormative and queer forms (Leong 1996).
9. In the film this song is picturised on a moving train (that can be read as phallic) making its journey through picturesque virginal countryside. See

Kabir (2003) for a further reading of the film's extensive use of Sufi mysticism as articulated within the film's narrative, and especially in its song and dance sequences, about the struggle for love amidst Indian state politics.

10. In the film the lead players are Aamir Khan, Akshaye Khanna, Preity Zinta and Saif Ali Khan.

11. A 'dark room' is a designated area within a gay and lesbian club often separate to the dance floor where people can enter and partake in or observe numerous kinds of sexual escapades.

12. See Prasad (1994) for an account of how Bollywood songs and dances are used in the context of Indian film censorship rules as standing in for the real thing. Prasad asserts that it is patriarchal authority that is promulgated in the scopophilia of these song and dance numbers.

13. Kavi, for example, describes the queerness of Bollywood star Dev Anand as possessing 'a strange effeminacy that bordered on the child-like' and 'had an innocuous sensuality about him that conspired to make his heroine into an oedipal figure' (Kavi 2000: 308).

14. I fully acknowledge here that this line of thought is brief and highly speculative and begs the need for further research to prove or disprove the claims being put forward in this instance about early Hindi cinema. Thus, by labelling the terms 'queer' and 'camp' in literal and metaphoric scare quotes (' ') I wish to draw attention to the possibilities in which these terms can and might not operate in ways that we understand their use in Western culture. This points towards a line of flight that requires us to think more about the similarities and dissimilarities of queer and camp cultures in South Asia and elsewhere.

15. I am thinking here of the films starring the stunt actress Nadia from the early thirties and onwards. See the interesting chapter by Rosie Thomas (2005) on 'Fearless Nadia' and her articulations with national identity formation during the thirties right to the fifties.

16. For example, Veena Oldenburg (1989) drawing on interviews with retired courtesans in Lucknow, India, argues that most courtesans, as well as many prostitutes, practised lesbianism (*chapat bazi*), considering heterosexuality to be work and not pleasure.

17. See for instance the Gay Bombay website www.gaybombay.cc.

18 The recent history of the struggle of the New York-based South Asian Lesbian and Gay Association (SALGA) to be included in the India Day Parade on the streets of Manhattan is a case in point. See Svati P. Shah, 'Out and Radical: New Directions for Progressive Organizing', http://www.samarmagazine.org/archive/article.php?id=60, date accessed 13 August 2004.

CHAPTER 6: BETWEEN AND BEYOND BOLLYWOOD AND HOLLYWOOD

1. Rosie Thomas (1985: 117–20) describes the elitist attitudes towards popular Hindi cinema from Western and Indian academics and film commentators

dating as far back as 1952; and Manjunath Pendakur (2003: 8–9) outlines the condescending and patronising tone accorded to Bollywood cinema in Western documentaries and media in Australia and in the US.

2. At least sections of the international media have acknowledged and referenced Luhrman's deployment of Bollywood aesthetics in *Moulin Rouge*. See for instance Chris England's article 'Never mind the length—feel the quality', *Guardian Unlimited*, 15 May 2002, http://film.guardian.co.uk/bollywood/story/0,11871,715739,00.html, date accessed September 2004.

3. Ashish Rajadhyaksha (2003) laments the arrival of corporate and foreign finance in Hindi cinema, suggesting that it is leading to a 'Bollywoodisation' of Indian popular cinema. He uses 'Bollywoodisation' to refer to the Hollywood-esque commodity-driven aspirations of some of Bollywood cinema's key producers, directors and actors that are keen to increasingly represent these desires through product placements, thereby changing the means of operation and pleasure of the cinema.

4. Lahore is the main film production centre of Pakistan and is popularly referred to as Lollywood. It makes films mostly in the languages of Urdu and Punjabi. On the history of Pakistani cinema, see Gazdar (1997).

5. For a more comprehensive list of documentaries, short and feature films with a South Asian diasporic focus, and also those made by South Asian diasporic film-makers up to the year 2002, see the filmography in Desai (2004: 265–72).

6. Alongside its international English-language release the film was also dubbed and released simultaneously in Hindi. The Hindi title of the film is *Balle Balle! Amritsar to LA* and it went on release in India, as well as in the mainstream cinemas of the West aimed at diasporic South Asians too.

BIBLIOGRAPHY

Adarsh, Taran (2004), 'Pakistan to screen Indian Films', http://www.indiafm.com/scoop/04/jul/0707indopak/index.shtml, date last accessed 8/7/04.

Aftab, Kaleem (2002), 'Brown: The New Black! Bollywood in Britain', *Critical Quarterly*, 44 (3): 88–98.

Ahmed, Akbar (1992), 'Bombay Films: The Cinema as Metaphor for Indian Society and Politics', *Modern Asian Studies*, 26 (2): 289–320.

Alfonsi, Laurence (1999), 'Cinematic Sociology vis-à-vis Social Change: The American Response to Film Maker F. Truffaut', *Free Inquiry in Creative Sociology*, 27 (1): 3–8.

Appadurai, Arjun (1990), 'Disjuncture and Difference in the Global Cultural Economy', *Public Culture*, 2 (2): 295–310.

—— (1996), *Modernity at Large: Cultural Dimensions of Globalisation*. Minneapolis and London: University of Minnesota Press.

Bailey-Grant, Brigit (2004), 'A Reel Woman: Gurinder Chadha', *Zee Magazine*, Winter, pp. 108–12. London: Profile Pursuit Ltd.

Bamzai, Kaveree (2003), 'Brave New Directions: A New Generation of Actors, Directors and Producers Redefine Hindi Cinema', *India Today*, 9 September, pp. 34–47. Harrow: Living Media International Ltd.

Banaji, Shaku (2004), A Qualitative Analysis of Young Hindi Film Viewers' Readings of Gender, Sexuality and Politics On- and Off-Screen. Unpublished Ph.D Thesis. Institute of Education: University of London.

Bandyopadhyay, S. (ed.) (1993), *Indian Cinema: Contemporary Perceptions from the Thirties*. Jamshedpur: Celluloid Chapter.

Barnouw, Erik and S. Krishnaswamy (1980), *Indian Film*. New York: Oxford University Press.

Baty, S. Paige (1995), *American Monroe: The Making of a Body Politic*. London, Berkeley, California: University of California Press.

Bhabha, Homi (1990), *Nation and Narration*. London: Routledge.

—— (1994), *The Location of Culture*. London: Routledge.

Bhattacharyya, Gargi and John Gabriel (1994), 'Gurinder Chadha and the *Apna* Generation', *Third Text*, 27: 55–63.

Bhuchar, Sudha (1996), 'Indian Cinema: A History of Presence in Britain', *Libaas International*, 9 (2): 88–90.

Bordwell, David and Kristin Thompson (2001), *Film Art: An Introduction*. Sixth edition. New York: McGraw-Hill.

Branigan, Tania (2004), 'My Film is Part of the Peace Process', *Guardian Unlimited*, http://www.guardian.co.uk/arts/fridayreview/story 0,12102, 1146453,00.html, date last accessed 13/2/04.

Breckenridge, Carol (1995), *Consuming Modernity Public Culture in a south Asian World*, Minnesota: University of Minnesota Press.

Brooker, Will and Deborah Jermyn (2002), *The Audience Studies Reader*. London: Routledge.

Bulmer, Herbert (1933), *Movies and Conduct*. New York: Macmillan.

Chakravarty, Sumati (1996), *National Identity in Indian Popular Cinema: 1947–1987*. New Delhi: Oxford University Press.

Chaterjee, Partha (1986), *Nationalist Thought and the Colonial World: A Derivative Discourse?*, London: Zed Books.

Chaudhary, Vivek (1998), 'Film's Greatest Fans', *The Guardian*, 4 December, p. 12

Chopra, Anupama (1997a), 'Bollywood: Crisis of Flops', *India Today*, 10 November. Harrow: Living Media International Ltd.

—— (1997b), 'Bye-Bye Bharat', *India Today*, 1 December, pp. 53–54. Harrow: Living Media International Ltd.

—— (1998), 'The Fast Fade Out', *India Today*, 29 June, pp. 46–47. Harrow: Living Media International Ltd.

—— (2003), *Dilwale Dulhaniya Le Jayenge—The Brave-hearted Will Take the Bride*. London: BFI Publishing.

Chow, Rey (1998), 'Film and Cultural Identity', in John Hill and Pamela Church Gibson (eds), *The Oxford Guide to Film Studies*, pp. 169–74. Oxford: Oxford University Press.

Ciecko, Anne (2001), 'Superhit Hunk Heroes for Sale: Globalization and Bollywood's Gender Politics', *Asian Journal of Communication*, 11 (2): 121–43.

Cohen, Lawrence (1995a), 'Holi in Banaras and the Mahaland of Modernity', *Gender and Lesbian Quarterly*, 2 (4): 399–424.

—— (1995b), 'The Pleasures of Castration: The Postoperative Status of Hijras, Jhankas, and Academics', in Paul Abramson and Steven Pinkerton (eds), *Sexual Nature Sexual Culture*. Chicago and London: University of Chicago Press.

Cook, David (1996), *A History of Narrative Film*. Third edition. New York: Norton.

Cook, Pam (1999), *The Cinema Book*. Second edition. London: BFI.

D'Mello, Pamela (2003), 'US-Based Digital Studio to Branch out in Goa', *Asian Age*, 18 June, p. 4.

Das Gupta, Chidananda (1981), *Talking about Films*. New Delhi: Orient Longman.

——— (1991), *The Painted Face: Studies in India's Popular Cinema*. New Delhi: Orient Longman.

Deleuze, Gilles (1995), 'On Control and Becoming', in *Negotiations*, translated by Martin Joughin. New York: Columbia University Press.

Deleuze, Gilles and Guattari (1983), *On the line*, translated by John Johnston. New York: Semiotexte.

Denzin, Norman (1991), *Images of Postmodern Society: Social Theory and Contemporary Cinema*. London: California; New Delhi: Sage Publications.

——— (1995), *The Cinematic Society: The Voyeur's Gaze*. London: California; New Delhi: Sage Publications.

Derrida, Jacques (1983), *Disseminations*, translated by Barbara Johnson. Chicago: University of Chicago Press.

Desai, Jigna (2004), *Beyond Hollywood: The Cultural Politics of South Asian Diasporic Film*. New York: Routledge.

Dissanayake, Wimal (ed.) (1944), *Colonialism and Nationalism in Asia*. Indiana: Indiana University Press.

Dissanayake, Wimal and Malti Sahai (1992), *Sholay: A Cultural Reading*. New Delhi: Wiley Eastern Ltd.

Dowd, James (1999), 'Waiting for Louis Prima: On the Possibility of a Sociology of Film', *Teaching Sociology*, 14 (4): 324–42.

Dubey, Bharti K. (2003), 'Bollywood Sans Frontiers', *Asian Age*, 4 July, p. 9.

Dudrah, Rajinder (2001), British South Asian Identities and the Popular Cultures of British Bhangra Music, Bollywood Films, and Zee TV in Birmingham. Unpublished Ph.D Thesis, Department of Cultural Studies and Sociology, University of Birmingham.

——— (2002a), 'Vilayati Bollywood: Popular Hindi Cinema-Going and Diasporic South Asian Identity in Birmingham (UK)', in *Javnost: Journal of the European Institute for Culture and Communication*, 9 (1): 9–36.

——— (2002b), 'Drum N Dhol: British Bhangra Music and Diasporic South Asian Identity Formation', *European Journal of Cultural Studies*, 5 (3): 363–83.

——— (2004), 'Diasporicity in the City of Portsmouth (UK): Local and Global Connections of Black Britishness', *Sociological Research Online*, 9 (2), http://www.socresonline.org.uk/9/2/dudrah.html.

——— (2005), 'Zee TV: Diasporic Non-terrestrial Television in Europe', *South Asian Popular Culture*, 3 (1): 33–47.

Dwyer, Rachel (2000), *All You Want Is Money, All You Need Is Love: Sex and Romance in Modern India*. London: Cassell.

Dyer, Richard (1979), *Stars*. London: British Film Institute.

Ellis, John (1982), *Visible Fictions: Cinema, Television, Video*. London: Routledge and Kegan Paul.

Feuer, Jane (1993), *The Hollywood Musical*. Second edition. London: Macmillan.

Ganti, Tejaswini (2004), *Bollywood: A Guidebook to Popular Hindi Cinema*. New York: Routledge.

Garga, Bhagwan Das (1996), *So Many Cinemas: The Motion Picture in India*. Mumbai: Eminence Designs.

Gazdar, Mushtaq (1997), *Pakistan Cinema:1947–1997*. Pakistan: Oxford University Press.

Gillespie, Marie (1995), *Television, Ethnicity and Cultural Change*. London: Routledge.

Goffman, Erving (1959), *The Presentation of Self in Everyday Life*. Doubleday: Garden City, New York.

Gokulsing, K. Moti and Wimal Dissanayake (1998), *Indian Popular Cinema: A Narrative of Cultural Change*. Stoke-on-Trent: Trentham Books.

Goldenberg, S. and V. Dodd (1998), 'The Indians Are Coming', *The Guardian*, 3 September, p. 7.

Gomery, Douglas (1998), 'Hollywood as Industry', in John Hill and Pamela Church Gibson (eds), *The Oxford Guide to Film Studies*, pp. 245–54. Oxford: Oxford University Press.

Gopalan, Lalitha (2002), *Cinema of Interruptions: Action Genres in Contemporary Indian Cinema*. London: BFI Publishing.

Gopinath, Gayatri (2000), 'Queering Bollywood: Alternative Sexualities in Popular Indian Cinema', in Andrew Grossman (ed.), 'Queer Asian Cinema: Shadows in the Shade', Special Issue of *Journal of Homosexuality*, 39 (3 and 4): 283–97.

Grossman, Andrew (ed.) (2000), 'Queer Asian Cinema: Shadows in the Shade', Special Issue of *Journal of Homosexuality*, 39 (3 and 4).

Harvey, David (1989), *The Condition of Postmodernity*. Cambridge, Massachusetts: Blackwell.

Hayward, Susan (2000), *Cinema Studies: The Key Concepts*. London Routledge.

Hutnyk, John (1996), 'Media, Research, Politics, Culture', *Critique of Anthropology*, 16 (4): 417–28.

India Today (2004), 'Cover Story: Young Bollywood the Fast and Furious Generation that is Shaping the Movie Business', *India Today*, 2 August, pp.14–20. Harrow: Living Media International Ltd.

Jain and Chowdhury (1997), 'The Diaspora in Hindi Cinema', *India Today*, 1 July, pp. 27–28. Harrow: Living Media International Ltd.

Jameson, Frederic (1991), *Postmodernism or the Cultural Logic of Late Capitalism*. Durham, North Carolina: Duke University Press.

Jarvie, I.C. (1970), *Towards a Sociology of the Cinema: A Comparative Essay on the Structure and Functioning of a Major Entertainment Industry*. London: Routledge and Kegan Paul.

Jensen, Klaus Bruhn (ed.) (2002), *A Handbook of Media and Communications Research: Qualitative and Quantitative Methodologies*. London: Routledge.

Johnson, Edward (1987), *Bombay Talkies: Posters of the Indian Cinema*. West Midlands Area Museum Service Travelling Exhibition: Birmingham Central Library.

Joshi, Lalit (1998), 'Raider of the Heart', *India Today*, 19 October, pp. 20b–20f. Harrow: Living Media International Ltd.

Juluri, Vamsee K. (1999), 'Global Weds Local: The Reception of *Hum Aapke Hain Koun* in India', *European Journal of Cultural Studies*, 2 (2): 27–46.

Kabir, Ananya J. (2003), 'Allegories of Alienation and Politics of Bargaining: Minority Subjectivities in Mani Ratnam's *Dil Se*', *South Asian Popular Culture*, 1 (2): 141–59.

Kasbekar, Asha (1996), 'An Introduction to Indian Cinema', in J. Nelmes (ed.), *An Introduction to Film Studies*, pp. 365–91. London: Routledge.

Katiyar, Arun (1994), 'Hindi Cinema: What the Stars Don't Foretell', *India Today*, 30 April, p. 74.

Kaul, G. (1998), *Cinema and the Indian Freedom Struggle*. New Delhi: Sterling.

Kaur, Raminder and Ajay Sinha (eds) (2005), *Bollyworld: Popular Indian Cinema through a Transnational Lens*. New Delhi: Sage Publications.

Kavi, Ashok Row (2000), 'The Changing Image of the Hero in Hindi Films', in Andrew Grossman (ed.), 'Queer Asian Cinema: Shadows in the Shade', Special Issue of *Journal of Homosexuality*, 39 (3 and 4): 307–12.

Kazmi, Fareed (1999), *The Politics of India's Conventional Cinema: Imaging a Universe, Subverting a Multiverse*. New Delhi, Thousand Oaks, London: Sage Publications.

Kazmi, Nikhat (1998), *The Dream Merchants of Bollywood*. New Delhi: UBS Publishers.

Klobah, Loretta Collins (2003), 'Pakistani Englishness and the Containment of the Muslim Subaltern in Ayub Khan-Din's Tragi-Comedy Film *East is East*', *South Asian Popular Culture*, 1 (2): 91–108.

Kuhn, Annette and Jackie Stacey (eds) (1999), *Screen Histories: A Screen Reader*. Oxford: Clarendon Press.

Larkin, Brian (1997), 'Indian Films and Nigerian Lovers: Media and the Creation of Parallel Modernities', *Africa*, 67 (3): 406–40.

Leong, Russell (ed.) (1996), *Asian American Sexualities: Dimensions of the Gay and Lesbian Experience*. London: Routledge.

Maira, Sunaina Marr (2002), *Desis in the House: Indian American Youth Culture in New York City*. Philadelphia: Temple University Press.

Malcolm, Derek (1989), 'The Million Hankie Weepie', *The Guardian: Screen*, 19 January, p. 11.

Mankekar, Purnima (1999), 'Brides Who Travel: Gender, Transnationalism, and Nationalsim in Hindi Film', *Positions*, 7 (3): 731–61.

Manuel, Peter (1993), *Cassette Culture: Popular Music and Technology in North India*. Chicago: University of Chicago Press.

Marks, Laura (2000), *The Skin of the Film*. Durham: Duke University Press.

Marre, Jeremy and Hannah Charlton (1985), *Beats of the Heart: Popular Music of the World*. London: Pluto Press.

Mills, C. Wright (1959), *The Sociological Imagination*. New York: Oxford University Press.

Mishra, Vijay (2002), *Bollywood Cinema: Temples of Desire*. New York and London: Routledge.

Misra, Neelesh (2003), 'Quietly Pakistani Film Makers come to Bollywood for a Little Help', *Asian Age*, 21 June, p. 4.

Monaco, James (2000), *How to Read a Film*. Third edition. USA: Oxford University Press.

Moran, Albert (1998), 'Film Policy: Hollywood and Beyond', in John Hill and Pamela Church Gibson (eds), *The Oxford Guide to Film Studies*, pp. 365–70. Oxford: Oxford University Press.

Mukherjee, Bimal and Sunil Kothari (1995), *Rasa: The Indian Performing Arts in the Last Twenty-Five Years*. Calcutta: Anamika Kala Sangam Research and Publications.

Murphy, Robert (ed.) (2000), *British Cinema of the 90s*. London: BFI Publishing.

Nandy, Ashis (1998), *The Secret Politics of Our Desires: Innocence, Culpability and Indian Popular Cinema*. London: Zed Books.

Nayar, Sheila (2004), 'Invisible Representation: The Oral Contours of a National Popular Cinema', *Film Quarterly*, 57 (3): 13–23.

Neale, Stephen (2000), *Genre and Hollywood*. London: Routledge.

Network East (1997), 'Report on Asian Video Outlets and Video Piracy', November, BBC2 TV.

Oldenburg, Veena Talwar (1989), *The Making of Colonial Lucknow 1856–1877*. New Delhi: Oxford University Press.

Padmanabhan, Anil (2004), 'Special Effects: Hindi Films in the US', *India Today*, 12 July, pp. 34–35.

Patnaik, Priyadarshi (1997), *Rasa in Aesthetics: An Application of Rasa Theory to Modern Western Literature*. New Delhi: D.K. Print World.

Pendakur, Manjunath (2003), *Indian Popular Cinema: Industry, Ideology and Consciousness*. USA, New Jersey: Hampton Press Inc.

Pendergast, Christopher (1986), 'Cinema Sociology: Cultivating the Sociological Imagination through Popular Film', *Teaching Sociology*, 14 (4): 243–48.

Peterson, Ruth and L. Thurstone (1936), *Motion Pictures and the Social Attitudes of Children*. New York: Macmillan.

Power, Carla and Sudip Mazumdar (2000), 'Hooray for Bollywood: Billboards in South Africa advertising Indian films', *Newsweek International*, 28 February, accessed on-line at: http://www.diehardindian.com/news/news2802.htm, 19 October 2004.

Prasad, Madhava (1994), 'Cinema and the Desire for Modernity', *Journal of Arts and Ideas*, 25–26: 71–86.

―――― (1998), *Ideology of the Hindi Film: A Historical Construction*. New Delhi and Oxford: Oxford University Press.

Pratt, Mary Louise (1992), *Imperial Eyes: Travel Writing and Transculturation*. New York: Routledge.

Prince, Stephen (2004), 'The Emergence of Filmic Artifacts: Cinema and Cinematography in the Digital Era', *Film Quarterly*, 57 (3): 24–33.

Rai, Amit (1994), 'An American Raj in Filmistan: Images of Elvis in Indian Films', *Screen*, 35 (1): 51–77.

Raj, Dhooleka (1998), 'Book review of Marie Gillespie's *Television, Ethnicity and Cultural Change*' in *South Asian Social Researchers' Forum Newsletter*, 2:1. London: SASRF Publication.

Rajadhyaksha, Ashish (1998), 'Indian Cinema', in John Hill and Pamela Church Gibson (eds), *The Oxford Guide to Film Studies*, pp. 535–40. London: Oxford University Press.

—— (2003), 'The "Bollywoodization" of the Indian Cinema: Cultural Nationalism in a Global Arena', *Inter-Asia Cultural Studies*, 4 (1): 25–39.

Rajadhyaksha, Ashish and Paul Willemen (1994), *Encyclopaedia of Indian Cinema*. London and New Delhi: British Film Institute and Oxford University Press.

Rajchman, John (1977), 'Analysis in Power', *Semiotexte*, 2 (3): 45–58.

Ramachandran, T.M. (ed.) (1985), *Seventy Years of Indian Cinema, 1913–1983*, Bombay: Cinema India-International.

Rangacharya, Adya (1996), *The Natyasastra*, translated by Adya Rangacharya. New Delhi: Munshiram Manoharlal.

Rangoonwalla, Firoze (1975), *75 Year of Indian Cinema*. New Delhi: Indian Book Company.

—— (1982), *Indian Cinema: Past and Present*. New Delhi: Clarion.

Rao, R. Raj (2000), 'Memories Pierce the Heart: Homoeroticism, Bollywood-style', in Andrew Grossman (ed.), 'Queer Asian Cinema: Shadows in the Shade', Special Issue of *Journal of Homosexuality*, 39 (3 and 4): 299–306.

Rao, Suvarnalata (2000), *Acoustical Perspective on Raga-Rasa Theory*. New Delhi: Munshiram Manoharlal.

Regan, Stephen (ed.) (1992), *The Politics of Pleasure and Cultural Theory*. Buckingham: Open University Press.

Said, Edward (1978), *Orientalism*. London: Penguin.

Sassen, Saskia (1998), *Globalization and Its Discontents: Essays on the New Mobility of People and Money*. New York: New Press.

Schechner, Richard (1985), *Between Theatre and Anthropology*. Philadelphia: University of Pennsylvania Press.

—— (2001), 'Rasaesthetics', *TDR: The Drama Review*, 45 (3): pp. 27–50.

Schroder, Kim et al. (2003), *Researching Audiences*. London: Arnold.

Sen, Soumik and S. Anusha (2003), 'The New Screen Teams', http://www.rediff.com/money/2003/jun/28spec.htm, date last accessed 3/12/04.

Shah, Nimesh (2003), 'Film industry in Co-production Mode', *Asian Age*, 19 March, p. 11.

Shakur, Tasleem and Karen D'Souza (2003), *Picturing South Asian Culture in English: Textual and Visual Representations*. Liverpool: Open House Press.

Sharma, Ashwani (1993), 'Blood, Sweat and Tears: Amitabh Bachchan, Urban Demi-God', in Pat Kirkham and Janet Thumim (eds), *You Tarzan: Masculinity, Movies and Men*, pp. 167–180. London: Lawrence and Wishart.

Sharma, Sanjay (1996), 'Noisy Asians or Asian Noise?', in Sanjay Sharma, Johan Hutnyk and Ashwani Sharma (eds), *Dis-Orienting Rhythms: The Politics of the New Asian Dance Music*, pp. 32–57. London: Zed Books.

Sharma, Sanjay, John Hutnyk and Ashwani Sharma (eds) (1996), *Dis-Orienting Rhythms: The Politics of the New Asian Dance Music*. London: Zed Books.

Shilling, Chris (1993), *The Body and Social Theory*. London, Newbury Park and New Delhi: Sage Publications.

Smith, Daniel (2003), 'Deleuze on Bacon: Three Conceptual Trajectories', in Gilles Deleuze (ed.), *Francis Bacon: The Logic of Sensation*. Minnesota: University of Minnesota Press.

Smith, Neil (1998), 'Giuliani Time: The Revanchist 1990s', *Social Text*, pp. 1–20.

Stacey, Jackie (1993), *Star Gazing: Hollywood Cinema and Female Spectatorship*. London: Routledge.

Swingewood, Alan (1977), *The Myth of Mass Culture*. London: Macmillan.

Thomas, Rosie (1985), 'Indian Cinema: Pleasures and Popularity', *Screen*, 26 (3–4), pp. 116–31.

—— (2005), 'Not Quite (Pearl) White: Fearless Nadia, Queen of the Stunts', in Raminder Kaur and Ajay Sinha (eds), *Bollyworld: Popular Indian Cinema through a Transnational Lens*, pp. 35–69. New Delhi: Sage Publications.

Tinkcom, Matthew and Amy Villarejo (eds) (2001), *Key Frames: Popular Cinema and Cultural Studies*. London and New York: Routledge.

Tololyan, Kachig (1996), 'Rethinking Diaspora(s): Stateless Power in the Transnational Moment', *Diaspora*, 5 (1): 3–36.

Tudor, Andrew (1974), *Images and Influence: Studies in the Sociology of Film*. London: George Allen and Unwin.

—— (1998), 'Sociology and Film', in John Hill and Pamela Church Gibson (eds), *The Oxford Guide to Film Studies*, pp. 190–94. Oxford: Oxford University Press.

Turner, Bryan (1992), *Regulating Bodies: Essays in Medical Sociology*. London: Routledge.

Turner, Graeme (1998), 'Cultural Studies and Film', in John Hill and Pamela Church Gibson (eds), *The Oxford Guide to Film Studies*, pp. 195–201. Oxford: Oxford University Press.

Tyrrell, Heather (1998), 'Bollywood in Britain', *Sight and Sound*, August, pp. 20–22.

Uberoi, Patricia (1998), 'The Diaspora Comes Home: Disciplining Desire in *DDLJ*', *Contributions to Indian Sociology*, 32 (2): 305–36.

—— (2001), 'Imagining the Family: An Ethnography of Viewing Hum Aapke Hain Koun…!', in Rachel Dwyer and Christopher Pinney (eds), *Pleasure and the Nation: The History, Politics and Consumption of Public Culture in India*, pp. 309–351. New Delhi: Oxford University Press.

Unnikrishnan, Rajesh and Nimesh Shah (2003), 'Film Industry Divided on Institutional Financing', *Asian Age*, 17 March, p. 11.

Unnithan, Sandeep (2004), 'In its True Colours', *India Today*, pp. 44–46. Harrow: Living Media International Ltd.

Valicha, Kishore (1988), *The Moving Image: A Study of Indian Cinema*. Bombay: Orient Longman.

Vasudev, Aruna and Philipe Lenglet (eds) (1983), *Indian Cinema Super Bazaar*. New Delhi: Vikas Publishing House.

Vasudevan, Ravi (1989), 'The Melodramatic Mode and Indian Commercial Cinema', *Screen*, 30 (3).

Vasudevan, Ravi (2000), *Making Meaning in Indian Cinema*. New Delhi: Oxford University Press.

Virdi, Jyotika (2003), *The Cinematic Imagination: Indian Popular Films as Social History*. New Brunswick, New Jersey and London: Rutgers University Press.

Waterhouse, David (ed.) (1998), *Dance of India*. Mumbai: Popular Prakashan.

Waugh, Thomas (2001), 'Queer Bollywood, or I'm the Player You're the Naïve One: Patterns of Sexual Subversion in Recent Indian Popular Cinema', in Matthew Tinkcom and Amy Villarejo (eds), *Key Frames: Popular Cinema and Cultural Studies*, pp. 280–97. London and New York: Routledge.

Wollen, Peter (1969), *Working Papers on the Cinema: Sociology and Semiology*. London: British Film Institute.

INDEX

ABOUT THE AUTHOR

Rajinder Kumar Dudrah is Lecturer in Screen Studies, University of Manchester, and was earlier Research Fellow in Sociology, University of Portsmouth. He has researched and published extensively on film, media and cultural studies in international journals.